Matthew M

Feeding and Sheltering Backyard Birds

All you need to know about proper food and feeding,
housing and care throughout the year

With a special section on help with nesting

Color photographs by Steven Maslowski and
illustrations by Michele Earle-Bridges

BARRON'S

Copyright © 1990 by Barron's Educational Series, Inc.

All inquiries should be addressed to:
Barron's Educational Series, Inc.
250 Wireless Boulevard
Hauppauge, NY 11788

International Standard Book No. 0-8120-4252-2

Library of Congress Catalog Card No. 89-18092

Library of Congress Cataloging-in-Publication Data

Vriends, Matthew M., 1937-
    Feeding and sheltering backyard birds: all you need to know about proper food and feeding, housing, and care throughout the year with a special section on help with nesting/Matthew M. Vriends ; color photographs by Steven Maslowski and illustrations by Michele Earle-Bridges.
        p.   cm.
    Includes bibliographical references.
    ISBN 0-8120-4252-2
    1. Birds, Attracting of—North America. 2. Bird watching—North America. 3. Birds—North America. I. Title.
QL676.5.V75   1990
639.9′782097—dc20   89-18092
                                                      CIP

PRINTED IN CHINA

456   4900   987

About the author

Matthew M. Vriends is a Dutch-born biologist/ornithologist who holds a collection of advanced degrees, including a PhD in zoology. Dr. Vriends has written more than 80 books in three languages on birds and other animals; his detailed works on parrotlike birds and finches are well known. He has traveled extensively in South America, the United States, Africa, Australia, and Europe to observe and study birds in their natural environment. Dr. Vriends and his family live near Cincinnati, Ohio. He is the author of two of Barron's Pet Owner's Manuals, *Lovebirds* and *Pigeons*, and of *New Bird Handbook* and *New Cockatiel Handbook*.

Photo credits

The eastern bluebird and the American goldfinch by Gary Ellis; all other photos by Steven Maslowski, Maslowski Wildlife Productions.

Front cover: The ruby-throated hummingbird.
Inside front cover: The house wren.
Inside back cover: The northern cardinal.
Back cover: The house finch.

For Leela Dwivedi, MD
Soyons fidèles à nos faiblesses.

Contents

Contents

Introduction

I was fortunate enough to grow up surrounded by plants and animals. Both my father and uncle were biologists, so it is not surprising that even at an early age I accompanied them on their field trips to observe and study the wonders of nature. From the start, birds loomed large on my interest scale, and I have countless memories of lying on my stomach, clad in shorts, on sand or grass or hay, bird watching, while all sorts of creepy crawlers marched across my legs. Some of them stung me too!

By the time my shorts gave way to long corduroy pants (which I would tuck into watertight boots, just as my father and uncle did), I could recognize the vast majority of bird species we would spy on—some 250 in all—by sound, silhouette, and flight behavior. My enthusiasm bordered on the fanatic as I delved into their breeding habits. Before I was half way through my secondary education, I had started a biology club, with its members devoted to spending their weekends and vacations bird watching or frantically scurrying after frogs, snakes, salamanders, or stickle-backs, bringing the less agile creatures back to be observed by still more Homo sapiens through the four large aquariums that our biology department boasted. Both my father and uncle taught in that department, and I must say, they did not make things easy for me. In fact, to this day I am convinced that they made me work much harder than my classmates!

Located some five miles from where I grew up in the Netherlands is the peaceful little town of Valkenswaard, which means "home of the falcons." For over five centuries, and now under the enthusiastic leadership of Mr. J. de Mooy, the falconers have practiced their knightly art. I could listen to their tales for hours, and on a couple of occasions I was lucky enough to be allowed to accompany them, albeit with a trembling heart, to watch the magnificent wild hawks and falcons hunt doves and rabbits.

During my sixteenth year my father decided to show me the fascinating caves at Lascaux in France. Among other reasons, he wanted to reveal to me that the study of birds reaches far back into unknown times. The painted scene that stretched before me showed a bird on a branch and to its right, a wounded bison staring at a sorcerer sporting the mask of a bird. The true meaning of this presentation continues to elude man and is actually quite different from the other art in the caves. In any event, we can conclude that man and bird have had a strong impact on each other since time immemorial.

For those interested in antiques, a vast array of bird motifs can be discovered in the craftsmanship of old wood carvings, old weapons, silver candelabra, and jewelry. Try reading old fables, myths, and legends, and studying exotic cultures—time and again you will come across a bird theme. Think, for example, of the Egyptian god Horus, who is represented with the head of a falcon. Both in the wilds of nature and in the world of art, birds remain utterly important.

This beginner's manual will make things easy for you. We are going to study a number of birds that are regular visitors in your own garden. Naturally, our discussion will include such topics as suitable feeders, the most appropriate plant and shrubbery choices, nesting boxes, binoculars, photography, and the best method to help you correctly identify birds.

At this time I would like to thank Mrs. Terry Williams of East Northport, New York, for her invaluable assistance in the preparation of this book. I would like to express my gratitude once again to my wife, Mrs. Lucia Vriends-Parent, for her help and expertise with regard to ornithological issues. Finally, I would like to thank my dear friend, Arthur Freud of Smithtown, New York for his suggestions, corrections, and reading of the final manuscript.

Loveland, Ohio
Spring, 1990

Matthew M. Vriends

Where to Start

Birders Have Much to Endure

I live in a vastly varied natural area, just a stone's throw from a broad river that has both banks densely covered with thick underbrush and weeds. My own fairly large garden has many tall trees and dense bushes, and borders on a delightful piece of wild land as yet untouched by the ferocious and hungry teeth of the bulldozer. It is a veritable ShangriLa for all kinds of animals, and birds in particular seem to feel very safe there and find their little table always set for them.

When I bought the house in the spring, I could not wait to go through the property with a fine-tooth comb to discover which bird species I might encounter in my garden. On a Saturday morning I got up early, and in dark pants and T-shirt stealthily crept to the edge of that piece of wild land, with my binoculars slung around my neck, my guide book in hand. I selected what I thought would be a suitable spot, all very quietly, and got into a crouching position, binoculars in place, ready to scan the area for birds. Suddenly, I felt a tap on my shoulder, which completely startled me. Looking up, I first saw shiny buttons on a uniform, followed by the friendly but uncompromising face of (I found out soon enough) our local sheriff. Once I had managed to rise, rather awkwardly I might add, he came out with the usual question: What was I up to?

Obviously, if you want to become a field ornithologist, you cannot let such confrontations upset you too much, because they are a fairly common occurence. You will have regular contact with the police, gamekeepers, park keepers, rangers, foresters, and the like. I handled this event in the usual manner. I pointed to the binoculars and the bird guide and the spot I had chosen. Although this did not prove anything to him, he was content to let me have my say, and when I invited him to have a cup of coffee at "my house over there," he was convinced that I did not harbor any nefarious intentions and was only interested in birds. When I walked him back to his car, I asked him to pin a small notice on his office's bulletin board, just as a precaution, advising police officers and office personnel alike that I might often be found lurking behind bushes, binoculars around my neck, perhaps near bird feeders. All this in the hopes that it might put some concerned telephoning neighbors at peace.

If and when you decide to start studying and spying on birds outside your own property, save yourself a lot of headaches by being sure to carry valid identification. A membership card to a bird-watchers club can help explain apparently weird behavior. Be sure to have a valid permit for any places you visit that require one, and let any game warden, forester, or park ranger know when you arrive and how late or how long you plan to visit.

In our overly industrialized world, there is often very little area left for nature. The recent trend toward an ever growing concern for plants and animals is very encouraging. However, not everyone shares that interest. You may find that you receive an occasional suspicious glance, even when you are sitting in your own garden with your binoculars in hand. Talk to people if you have the opportunity to do so, and you will be amazed how fast the news will spread that there is a bird nut living in the neighborhood. Don't be surprised if a few weeks later you are suddenly seen as *the* expert, receiving calls day and night from people who think they have seen the most rare and exotic birds and want your verification, or who seek your advice on the care of a sparrow that has fallen out of its nest or a robin that has a broken wing after being hit by a car. Within a month you will be solidly the expert on birds and the rescuer of birds that had practically breathed their last. You owe it to yourself and to nature in general to know whereof you speak. Fortunately, you do not need to be a professional zoologist or ornithologist. Birding is open to anyone and is so fascinating you will, in no time at all, know a good deal about it, provided of course, that you are prepared to devote a little time and some effort to its study.

Where to Start

Millions of Americans are regularly involved in bird-watching, bird protection, and bird studies.

What's in a Name?

When I used to accompany my father on his favorite nature trails, he had me identify all the plants and animals not only by their local names (for me that was in Dutch) but also by their scientific names. As my father rightly pointed out to me, not every biologist or ornithologist speaks Dutch, but all will know the species you refer to if you use the scientific name. Those scientific names from Latin and Greek tell quite a lot about a plant or animal, as you can see from this list of Latin words prominent in scientific nomenclature.

communis: ordinary, common, found everywhere

vulgaris: universal, widespread habitat

cristatus: having a crest

domesticus: domestic, found near civilization

montanus: inhabits mountainous regions

guttatus: spotted, teardrop markings

major: larger

minor: smaller

Just as people have a family name and a given name, so do plants and animals, although these may have an additional name denoting the subspecies. In the nomenclature, a two-name identification is called *binary*, while a three-name identification is referred to as *ternary*. The scientific name starts with the family name, such as *Passer* in the house sparrow (*Passer domesticus domesticus*), which indicates the genus, followed by the species (*domesticus*), and followed by the geographical subspecies (in this case also *domesticus*). Quite often the third name is not mentioned, because classification of the subspecies is frequently based on such minute differences that positive identification in the wild is difficult, if not impossible. In most of the bird guide books the subspecies is simply omitted, unless there are clear differences discernible by the naked eye or with binoculars. Any given species includes all those birds that have an identical appearance, share the same living habits, and are mutually fertile, producing offspring that resemble themselves.

Binoculars

A good pair of prism-type binoculars should be included in the standard gear of any serious birder. Some birders experience headaches or eyestrain initially because they are not accustomed to spending a lot of time looking through binoculars. If you run into problems with your binoculars, have them checked and regulated by an optician. If you have difficulty focusing your eyes—after all, the object is likely to be small and constantly moving—you may need to give your eyes a little time to become trained. Using opera glasses is helpful, first peering at larger objects and later moving onto smaller ones. The next step might be to go to a park or zoo and practice looking first at large birds, such as swans, geese, or ducks, and then switching to smaller varieties, such as finches in aviaries. It will

Where to Start

not be long before you are able to focus on the smallest subjects.

That is the time to switch to field binoculars. There are a number of different opinions regarding which type of binoculars is best, but believe me, experienced ornithologists seldom use large or heavy ones. They may look impressive, but they are tiring to carry around and difficult to focus quickly. In addition, they quickly distort the image in view.

I myself work with fairly light, small, prism binoculars that focus very readily.

Because some habitats tend to be dark, like those deep in a forest or in a clump of closely growing trees, and because there are plenty of dark and somber days during the fall and winter, it is important to get binoculars with a good *relative brightness* factor.

It is important to understand the meaning of the two figures with which every pair of binoculars is marked. The numbers might be 7×50 or 8×30 or 10×40. The first figure indicates how many times the binoculars will enlarge an image, while the second figure is the diameter of the binoculars' objectives. The objectives are the lenses which you train onto an object, and the smaller these are, the less light they gather. So if the second figure is very low, say 16, the image you see through the glasses will be fairly dark. In this particular case, it will be practically impossible to distinguish colors on a dreary day, or at dawn or dusk, or deep in the woods.

When the enlargement potential (7, 8, or 10) is divided into the diameter of the objective (50, 30, or 40), the result equals the relative brightness mentioned earlier, which means the degree to which the image will be clear. For example, with binoculars that are 8×30, the relative brightness is: $30 \div 8 = 3.75$, or almost 4. Binoculars that are 8×40 have a relative brightness factor of 5, and 7×50 means a 7.14 factor. For birders, this factor should not be less than 4. Years of experience suggest that the ideal binoculars are 7×50 or 8×40. My personal preference is for 7×50.

The weight of binoculars has considerable in-

fluence on their price. Small, lightweight glasses do not run cheap, but once you have a good case of birder fever, which I guarantee you will catch more quickly than you would ever have thought, you will, no doubt, make frequent use of them. Besides, there is always your birthday or Christmas!

I strongly recommend the following binoculars: 7×50: Ideal for observing birds in your garden, considering the relative brightness factor. There are several heavy 7×50 glasses on the market, but our preference, of course, is for the lighter varieties, which do cost a little more.

8×40: Offer a slightly greater enlargement, although the relative brightness factor is somewhat reduced, and this may leave something to be desired on dark days or in thick forests.

10×40: Offer an even greater enlargement but are considerably more expensive. I particularly like to use these binoculars when my vantage point is likely to be far away from the subjects, as is sometimes the case with swans, geese, sandpipers, and the like. These glasses also lend themselves well to watching sea birds from a boat or backyard birds from your window during the winter.

12×65: These very strong glasses are excellent, although many birders find them a little too heavy and difficult to hold still. The relative brightness factor is also less than that of the prior models.

Above left: By the early 1900s the spectacular wood or Carolina duck neared extinction; it has made a remarkable comeback since.

Above right: The northern or common bobwhite is a gregarious species that has been introduced into many areas outside the USA.

Below left: The American kestrel is frequent in urban areas.

Below right: The ring-necked pheasant, originally from western Asia, has been introduced throughout Europe and North America.

Where to Start

Telescopes

Telescopes are suitable for observing and studying not only sea and beach birds, geese, swans, and ducks, but also backyard birds. They are generally purchased with a tripod. Because they are both costly and cumbersome, they are used primarily by experienced birders and professional ornithologists who want to watch birds for long periods of time from one location—so for the purpose of watching birds in the garden, they may be ideal.

If you decide to outfit yourself with a telescope, be sure that the lens enlarges between 20 × and 35 × and has an objective of at least 40 mm. But remember that the stronger the enlargement ability, the weaker the relative brightness factor and the smaller the focus. There are telescopes with zoom capabilities, but, needless to say, they don't go for nickels and dimes.

It is a good idea to select a definite place for mounting your telescope, perhaps on your patio or by a window, from which you can watch the busy lives of your feathered friends unfold.

Photographing Birds

Bird photography is generally frowned upon by the experts in the field and also by bird protection agency personnel. Now that practically all of us are in a position to buy sophisticated camera equipment, many people think that this is all that stands

Above left: The barn owl has an unmistakable heart-shaped face.
Above right: The great horned owl is found in all types of habitats.
Center left: The eastern screech owl is America's smallest eared owl.
Center right: The red-billed woodpecker, while in the air, catches many flying insects.
Below left: The downy woodpecker is fond of suet.
Below right: The northern or common flicker commonly feeds on ants.

between them and beautiful pictures. They see the gorgeous photographs in books and magazines, and figure that if they have the right equipment, they can duplicate that kind of quality. This line of thinking justifies fears in the field. Amateur photographers disrupt nests and foraging birds, to name just a couple of problems.

Anyone can, in theory, get involved with bird photography. Of course, photographers who have been involved for years with the life cycles and habits of birds have a clear advantage. However, the beginner who is not in a hurry and who wisely weighs the possibilities and situations that arise can reach a level that produces good results within just a few years. A thorough knowledge of the bird species you intend to photograph is as important as familiarity with the equipment you plan to use.

However, bird photography can do untold damage to bird species, and is most dangerous where vulnerable and rare species are concerned.

First of all, the bird photographer needs to become a peaceful hunter, his trophies being the black and white photograph, color slide, or film. Many a photographer, however, becomes simply a collector of bird pictures, whose sole goal is to capture a bird in print.

In the United States, as in many other countries, it is against the law to search for nests of protected species, and disrupting such a nest is punishable by law. And let's face it, nests with eggs or young have been photographed ad nauseum. A good photographer does not need a nest to get a species in print. Naturally, researchers specializing in the study of a specific species are going to include some nest photography, but their foremost interest is generally behavior. These researchers, of course, get to know their chosen species well, and no disruption occurs.

It is best, no doubt, to start in your own backyard, where the birds that come to visit your feeders are already somewhat accustomed to you. You cannot expect too much if you use an "Instamatic" type of camera, because it cannot take close ups. Besides that, the shutter speed is not fast enough for the quick motions of your winged subjects. I have achieved the best results with a 35mm single lens reflex camera. If your camera does not come equipped with a built-in light meter, you will need to buy one, but that should not break the bank. A standard 50mm lens will suffice also, but you will need a rigid tripod and a pneumatic release to use with it. For a beginner, I would recommend a medium speed film, such as 125 ASA black and white, or 64 ASA color. If you plan to take pictures when the weather is overcast, you may need a faster film. It may behoove you to buy your supplies from a reputable photo dealer, because you will not get any information apart from the price at your local supermarket.

Since you should initially restrict yourself to the taking of pictures at the bird feeder, or perhaps at a pond, it may be a good idea to set up a dummy camera on a pole a few days before you actually intend to take some shots. This way the birds will have a chance to become used to the strange object. Take an occasional stroll around the feeders and/or pond to help alleviate any fears your local birds might have.

The best time to photograph birds is early in the morning or late in the afternoon. When you want to start taking pictures, calmly but quickly exchange the dummy and pole for your tripod and camera. Generally, the birds will not react very

much. They may fly away for a few minutes but are usually back at the pond or feeder in no time at all. Place the camera about 2 feet (60 cm) from the feeder or pond. Set the shutter speed to no less than $\frac{1}{60}$ sec. The reading on your light meter will indicate the combination of shutter speed and f-stop (aperture) appropriate to the amount of light on the subject. All that remains is to focus. Don't be too chintzy with film when doing bird photography. Don't hesitate to take several shots and to experiment with various readings. Link up the pneumatic release and go stand quietly behind a tree or bush or even behind a window of your home or shed (the latter hiding place has much to recommend it). Don't be too trigger-happy, as the click of the camera will likely startle the birds, perhaps causing them to fly away. Exercise patience while your subject gets into the desired position. If you photograph regularly, most birds become used to it. Don't be surprised if a chickadee lands on your camera, contentedly preens its feathers, and looks you in the eye as if to say, "And *now* how do you intend to take a picture of me?"

Once you are thoroughly involved in this business of photographing birds, which also happens sooner than you think, it is time to buy a zoom lens. Personally, I think a 135 mm lens is ideal, because with this lens you won't need to come closer than 5 feet (1.5 m) from your subject.

Birds in the Garden

What Is a Garden Bird?

A garden is a totally artificial affair. It has been planned and laid out by people, who have attempted to create certain effects with flowers, bushes, and trees, many of which come from various other continents, and all aimed at pleasing humans. Birds and other animals that visit a garden originated in entirely different habitats, such as woodland and marshland. Actually, there is no such thing as a backyard bird in nature, and such terms as "garden birds" or "backyard birds" are artificial. This does not mean, however, that through the ages certain birds have not become typical garden and park birds, and this is totally in line with the natural progression of things. Because gardens and parks have been designed by people, a huge diversity of them has come into existence—so many people, so many minds. This offered a great opportunity for adjustment and modification to a number of different species. Many woodland birds, for example, have

Attracting wild birds to your yard requires a little time and planning. You must first provide for their basic needs: food, water, and proper shelter in a comfortable and protected environment.

shown through the years that they have not had the least bit of trouble spending their entire lives as backyard birds.

We cannot possibly come close to reviewing the yard and garden birds. If we were to line up all of the existing backyard birds and describe their origins, this book would be five times as thick. My only point is that by creating a particular pattern in our garden, we can attract a surprising diversity of birds in which we have a special interest. There are a number of species we can name that actually thrive better as garden birds than as woods or field birds. Several thrush species are good examples of original woods inhabitants that are far more successful as garden birds. Studies point out that garden thrushes raise about four times as many offspring as their cousins living along the edges of woodlands.

Sometimes the opposite is true. Many tits have a far more difficult time of it in a garden or park than in their original habitat, the coniferous woodlands or marshlands. This is especially the case when we take a look at the available nesting facilities and opportunities for efficient raising of the young. These birds generally have smaller clutches when living in gardens, and according to research, at least eight times as many young die because of insufficient availability of food. It also seems to me that the adult birds are somewhat smaller in build, due to the lack of a proper diet, and this causes a greater sensitivity to winter cold, and other climatic influences, resulting in a reduced longevity. The reason tits have more difficulties than, for example, thrushes, is obviously directly related to diet. Tits are primarily insecteaters—and there are plenty of insects in the coniferous forest—while thrushes, typical woodland-edge birds, eat berries and seeds in addition to insects and spiders—all readily available in a garden or park.

Then there are bird species like various woodpeckers that rely mainly on insects. The felling of woods and diseased trees greatly decreases their natural food sources, and they will have to scrounge around to see what they can find in gardens and parks. This is not a problem as long as there are not too many of them in the same area, because then there won't be enough to go around. In a situation like that, woodpeckers and other species become quite willing to try other items available on the menu. For a woodpecker, that might mean disposing of a nest of young tits after first cleverly clipping their nesting box.

What is a garden bird? From what we have discussed so far, it appears that there is no clear answer to that question. There are only a few birds, like the house sparrow, that have relied upon humans from time immemorial. The sparrow is the "domesticated wildbird" personified, among the backyard bird species. Meanwhile, people, whose numbers are growing at an alarming rate, have, unfortunately, claimed nature to be their rightful possession. Deforestation, the draining of swamps, ponds, rivers, and lakes are the order of the day, destroying the habitats of birds and hundreds of other animal species as well, with little consideration for the many forms of life which are thus threatened with extinction. Naturalists have, as we have seen, studied how various birds, once found only in the forests, have moved to parks, gardens, and towns. Some species, unable to move on when their habitats are encroached upon, totally vanish.

By converting our property to a real garden for birds, we may somewhat retard the spread of this devastating situation—for the sake of all species, including humans.

Garden Birds and the Law

We probably all agree that a well-designed garden can be an important contribution to wildlife conservation, especially in light of current environmental thinking. We do not necessarily have to give up or change much in the way of garden architecture already present. A person who likes a traditional garden can still help the cause of conservation by making a few adjustments.

It is possible that in some areas high populations of one or more species (such as house sparrows, starlings, feral pigeons, magpies, redwings, and common grackles) prevents other species from visiting your garden in search of food or to build a nest and rear young. Clearly, too many of one or more species is dangerous for the ecological balance of an area (in this case, your garden and its immediate surroundings). Obviously, it is not possible to simply shoot unwanted bird species, considering that all species are protected by law in both the United States and Canada. There are, of course, exceptions that apply to birds considered a pest or a quarry, but this still does not give us carte blanche with a gun. There are many limitations and restrictions concerning when, where, and how birds may be killed, and even by whom. For example, a landowner may remove starlings from his own land if they are damaging his crops, but he has to catch them in the act. On a piece of rented agricultural land, however, the landowner or a person he appoints to act on his behalf must first give permission before the unwanted birds may be shot. The hunting of game birds and waterfowl is regulated by yearly hunting quotas. A person who owns a large parcel of uncultivated land, perhaps with a natural water source, should be careful to clearly mark his or her property with warning signs attached to posts to prevent the unlawful killing of waterfowl or other species.

It pays to be informed about local laws. Consult your state conservation department, your library, local newspaper, or the Conservation Directory of the National Wildlife Federation for more information on this subject, which should certainly not be taken lightly.

Gardening for Birds

Planning the Garden

You have just bought a new house, but no landscaping has, as yet, been done. Some building ma-

Birds in the Garden

terials and other debris have been left lying around. The house is new, but the garden is a mess. Or perhaps you have an established garden. In either case, the question remains: Is your garden suitable for birds?

No matter what the situation, in no case is the random planting of trees, bushes, flowers, and grass the answer. The first step is to draw up a plan on paper. Use graph paper, because you will then be able to draw your plan to scale, provided, of course, that you measure everything out with care. If you have an established garden, you should outline all existing paths, lawns, flowerbeds, bushes, hedges, trees and tree groupings, any shed, garage, and, of course, the house. Not until all these details are down on paper should you proceed to the next step, which is to add planned improvements—again on paper, and initially in pencil. It may be advisable to have some soil samples tested to determine the type of soil in your garden. After all, not all plants do well in all types of soil. Checking whether trees and bushes presently growing in your garden are compatible with the soil type is also a good idea. There may be trees and bushes more suitable than the ones that you currently have. If your property has some sloping areas or some shady spots, the vegetation currently there should be evaluated as well. Before you complete your plans, you may want to think about the following points:

• Your landscaping plans should meet with the approval of all your family members. It would be wonderful to have your entire garden available for the use and lodging of birds, but realistically it is you and your family who must be happy with the final layout, not only the birds which come to visit.

• Consequently, your choice of trees and shrubs should provide plenty of food and shelter for the birds, and at the same time offer attractive and pleasant surroundings for you and your family members who will also use the garden.

• Any additional planting of vegetation should be done with an eye to adhering to a natural growth pattern. By this I mean that you should not become too much of a landscape architect, going for severe and unnatural lines. In a natural setting, as in the woods, you will see various levels of vegetation. There are basically four levels: 1) the ground, 2) the grasses and herbs, 3) the shrubs, and 4) the trees. Allow for a variation in heights. There are plenty of birds who prefer herbs and shrubs and seldom spend time up high in trees. Of course, the same applies the other way around.

• Keep in mind, when choosing plants, that some types will grow too high or too large for your garden or its layout. For example, a small garden that ends up with nothing but tall trees cannot be considered an aesthetic success. All you would see is tree trunks! If the undergrowth consists of nothing but herbs and grasses, a whole group of birds simply will not come to your garden.

• A few words about severe lines. In landscaping architecture these straight lines are all too prominent—just think of the straight paths and driveways, rectangular flowerbeds, and square lawns etc. In a natural setting you will not find this monotony of unnatural lines. If you maintain some irregular edges, a few curves here and there, the birds will undoubtedly feel more at home, and the garden will have a more natural look to it. Don't reject the idea of bringing about some elevation in your garden. I treat myself almost daily to some very pleasant bird observations made from a small rock formation in the southern corner of my garden. Even during the winter, when the flatter areas are covered with snow and few birds spend any time on the ground, I can generally find some activity on what we have come to call our rock plateau.

• Remember, when choosing plants, that many are seasonal. Keep in mind that it is important to know when they will flower and when they go to seed or have berries. Consult garden books to find out which plants will provide food for the birds (those that have flowers to attract edible insects or that have seeds or berries our birds will enjoy) as well as provide shelter for nesting and overnight quarters. Several hedge varieties do not lose their leaves until the spring, forming an excellent shelter for the winter, and cats, weasels, owls, and other enemies of small birds cannot do a lot of harm in such a hedge.

• If you are planning to add new trees or bushes to your garden, you may want to take a look in a natural park to see what appeals to you. Don't hesitate to use native species, but, of course, you cannot just dig them up and take them home. Your local nursery will, no doubt, be able to help you. These natives will attract a diversity of insects and other creepy crawlers known and enjoyed by the local bird population. They also offer seeds and other food with which the birds are familiar. In addition, the birds will be more likely to build a nest or spend the night in such a tree than in one foreign to them. Finally, the native trees will do better in your climate and in your soil.

The Unlandscaped Garden

It is easier to landscape a garden that has not yet had anything done to it than to modify a garden that is completely established. After all, when nothing has yet been done, you can realize all your plans from scratch. Either way, the garden represents a fairly costly investment, and you should keep this in mind.

If your property has some wild areas that have been like that for a number of years, with some dense shrubbery and grasses, ferns, wild flowers, and especially nettles, which always attract a lot of insects, and perhaps a few trees with full and dense crowns, you may want to maintain a few of these remotely situated pieces of untouched nature. Of course, you will need to be careful that any flowerbeds and rockgardens you build are not immediately adjacent to these wilderness areas with their spreading weeds and grasses. A little piece of your own natural park is an ideal shelter and sleeping place for many birds and other animal species, particularly if it has some dense bushes, lots of undergrowth, and full trees. High grass, ivy, and weeds have their place as well, since these attract many insects and offer good hiding places for the birds. Lamb's quarters and thistles are among the weeds that are popular with seedeating birds like goldfinches, evening grosbeaks, house finches, and to a lesser degree, purple finches and red cardinals.

Special attention should be paid to such details as ensuring that trees and bushes are planted not only to provide shelter from the cold or relief from the sun, but also to provide nest-building opportunities. Many bird species will select a place in a bush or somewhat bare tree branch during the spring from which to perform a spring concert. It is also important that the birds have water available. Plan the layout of your garden in such a manner that a certain multi-level effect is created. Starting at the front, border a lawn with low flowers, followed by low shrubs and bushes, followed by smaller and then taller trees. The whole should have a natural, terraced look to it. In the wild, nature stays away from stark, straight lines, and so should we.

The most important point to keep in mind during the planning of the layout is that it afford a good view from the house so you can observe and study the birds. Keep this in mind when you go to hang up nesting boxes, select places for birdbaths, build a pond, or choose locations for bird tables, which you will supply with a rich assortment of food.

If you are planning to build a vegetable garden for your own use, choose a location where the birds will be least likely to come, since you would undoubtedly prefer to keep the birds away from this area. If keeping the birds away seems unlikely, you may want to install some kind of netting (available at your local nursery) to protect your crops from the birds.

If your property does not hold much potential—in plain English, a postage-sized lot—it is still possible to attract a number of backyard birds by planting a few trees and bushes, to which many species are particularly attracted. Some that come to mind are cotoneaster, mountain ash, and crabapple. I know a bird fancier who lives in Manhattan and has only a balcony, and a small one at that. Nevertheless, he has a couple of potted cotoneaster and mountain ash as well as a birdbath and bird feeder.

Birds in the Garden

As a result, he thoroughly enjoys the bird life that passes by his home. In the two years that he has lived there, he has observed some thirty-seven different species.

Regardless of what you have and what you are planning to do, draw all your plans on paper first. Use a piece of graph paper to make drawing to scale easier. Talk to a local nursery manager: "How high does this species get?" "Will this species do well in my soil?" "Does this bush bear edible berries?" Browse through some garden books that give examples of garden layouts and the maintenance each requires, all spelled out in simple terms. In your sketch don't forget to add a pond and a good sized lawn if property dimensions will allow. A sizeable lawn will give the birds time to look things over, offering good visibility of dangers all around, and giving them a feeling of safety. It also provides a great place for building a pond, as well as a good location for feeders and water fountains. Many birds enjoy spending time on a lawn. It is like a table already set for them, with its numerous insects, ants, grubs, and earthworms. Earthworms are really up there in importance, as far as birds are concerned (see page 18). If you have any willow and cherry trees, don't be too hasty in removing all the fallen leaves in the autumn, because they are big favorites with earthworms, which, in turn, will be appreciated by your backyard birds. Perhaps leaving a portion of the leaves until the spring is a possibility for you.

As mentioned earlier, try to stay away from severe, straight lines when planning your garden. One straight line is an exception to this rule—a hedge. Perhaps some bush groupings, trees, or rock formations can be bordered by a hedge. If you keep a compost pile, this can be hidden behind the hedge. Your best choices for a hedge would be hazel, thorn, holly, or hawthorn. A hedgerow will be a big reason for the majority of the birds named in this book to come and stay with you. A hedge is great for shelter, sleeping, nesting, and provides all kinds of food as well. Many thrush varieties indulge themselves in the fall and early winter with berry pulp,

while all kinds of finches and tits enjoy the pips in the droppings. Spiders and all sorts of insects hibernate in the dormant shrubs and sooner or later provide a beak-full of food for some bird on the hunt.

Although I personally find rhododendrons breathtakingly beautiful, they are not particularly suited for a bird garden because the protection provided by the leafy "roof" is too open and too large, so that shelter against the cold and the wind is insignificant. Furthermore, not many insects are drawn toward this plant, so that it is not very important as a food source.

If you are planning to plant any fruit trees, you can protect these from snacking birds with netting. Don't forget to leave a few pieces of fruit for the birds after your have removed the netting and the better part of your crop.

Don't be too precise in removing dead or damaged parts of any trees and bushes you plan to plant. Check with your nursery to see if there will be any harm in leaving some of those parts, since they can provide a wealth of insects. Later, when you have some older trees or when some branches or trunks in your wilderness are riddled with holes, don't subject them to your chainsaw immediately. You can convert such a rotting tree trunk to a piece of garden sculpture by planting a clematis next to it. In no time flat, your climbing plant will have covered that ugly piece of wood with a glorious blanket of flowers.

Adapting An Established Garden

Your first step should be to check if most of the trees and shrubs in your garden are natives. If not, see if you still have room to add some, being sure to use a ground-plan. Generally, willow, elm, birch, and ash do well in almost all types of soil and climates. They grow fast and attract a rich assortment of birds. Don't be too quick with an axe or saw. Old trees often have holes that house edible insects, besides being used by many breeding birds (woodpeckers, chickadees). I suppose you will have rec-

17

Birds in the Garden

ognized the basic theme by now. We want to encourage a garden that is appealing to birds, which is to say, a garden that offers safety, has nesting possibilities, and provides dining facilities all year round. It is not just a matter of food that we provide, but, more importantly, food that the birds can glean between twigs and find on the ground.

Because no birds are alike in character or behavior, we, as bird fanciers, should provide them with as varied a choice of plants as is possible, allowing them to form their territories in the spring. The forming of territorial rights, incidentally, can be fascinating to watch. Quite often birds feel a certain pull toward specific trees and bushes, so that it follows that the greater the variety of trees, the greater the variety of birds we can expect. An established garden gives us the opportunity to add some hedges (see page 17), and a multi-level look of low and medium-sized plants in front of tree groups. Don't forget to make room for a generous lawn, in which you might place a pond surrounded by some flowerbeds and perhaps a hedge behind it with some smaller bushes, all to be seen from your window. Perhaps you may still be able to add some shrubs around your house, interspersed with flowerbeds. Ivy trained on your house, garage, or shed, attracts many birds.

The garden with tall trees will attract primarily forest-oriented birds like tanagers, thrushes, nuthatches, cedar waxwings, evening grosbeaks, northern cardinals, and purple finches, to name just a few. See if it is possible to add a lawn, even if it means sacrificing a couple of trees. An open space gives us the opportunity to create a terraced effect: undergrowth, shade-loving bushes, small trees. The present trees may need to have their lowest branches (probably dead anyway) removed. If you have mostly evergreens in your garden, consider replacing a few with deciduous trees. Don't forget the pond.

In the garden that has primarily shrubs and lawn we are likely to find American goldfinches, mockingbirds, thrushes, bluebirds, catbirds, northern cardinals, northern flickers, and yellow-bellied sapsuckers, to name a few from a much longer list. Begin by planting shrubs and vines around the house, garage, and/or shed, if there is space, without interfering with the view from your windows. Next plant a few fast-growing trees, such as red maple or pin oak, in the lawn, remembering the view from your window. If you happen to have a tall tree already growing in your garden, you might want to plant a few smaller trees, preferably of the same type, nearby. If there are too many shrubs, you may want to remove a few and replace them with fast growing trees. Remember to keep an eye on the lines you are creating, keeping them natural, not stiff and straight. A good location for your pond, easily observed from your home, is important. Add a few flowerbeds containing perennials and annuals that bear seed heads (aster, goldenrod, chrysanthemum, and various grasses such as pampas, tufted hair, and little blue stem) plus a rock formation to transform this type of garden into a veritable birds' paradise.

Lastly we come to the small garden, common in urban neighborhoods. Here again, a pond in the lawn, no matter how small, is essential. Around the lawn we could place first some lower and then higher shrubs and trees, interspersed with an occasional flowerbed. Should a pond really not fit in the allotted space, a birdbath, available in various sizes, is the next best thing. Even if you live in an apartment with just a balcony or a terrace, you can have flower boxes and potted trees and bushes. Many birds are quick to spot a little green in the concrete jungle, and if you scientifically approach the problem of which food to offer, you can expect various birds to visit year-round. There are also window bird feeders on the market, so it is possible to receive bird visitors even if you have no garden or balcony at all.

Worming Grounds

When I first began to bird-watch, I was fascinated by our blackbird (*Turdus merula*) when he

was worming on dewy mornings. At first I was totally convinced that our blackbird could actually
hear the earthworms digging, as evidenced by the
way he held his head to one side. Then my father
pointed out that since the eyes of our blackbird, as
well as those of all other birds, are situated at the
sides of its head, its field of vision is at right angles
to ours. In addition, he told me that birds cannot
move their eyes in their sockets, so that they have
to cock their heads so they can carefully inspect
the ground at their feet.

As a young boy I also learned how to catch
worms for fishing bait. You stick a shovel into the
earth and tap against the handle and pole. As if by
magic the worms appear! As children, we used to
say that the worms thought that there were moles
in hot pursuit and in panic wished to flee to the
surface. This illusion was also quickly shattered—
that happens when your father is a biologist—as he
quickly offered a different reason, with which we
were not particularly happy. Actually, it is the un-
derground vibrations that bring the earthworms to
the surface. It took me until the first year of my
secondary schooling, however, to realize that
earthworms have more importance than supplying
fishing bait and a welcome snack for birds. Worms
are absolutely essential to the soil, so never kill
them. Their burrowing helps fertilize and drain the
soil and aerate the grass roots. Our motto should
be: No lawn without worms. If you consult a book
on the maintenance of lawns, you will undoubtedly
discover this after the first hundred pages or so.

I like to run the lawn sprinklers during the evening, particularly after a hot day. This not only benefits the lawn, but brings the worms to the surface.
This in turn invites the birds for an enthusiastic
worm hunt.

Water, the Source of All Life

Just like humans, birds cannot go long without
water. It is necessary for the proper functioning of
the body. As you probably know, birds do not tran-
spire. Nevertheless, they do lose water through ex-
cretion. There is some water in the food they eat,
although unripe seeds would never contain enough
moisture to sustain life, and the majority of their
water is taken in through drinking. Birds that spend
a great deal of their time in the crowns of trees or
dense shrubbery take in quite a lot of moisture from
dewdrops and raindrops that cling to the leaves and
twigs, but this will never suffice. Consequently,
most birds will visit a pond, pool, river, or lake to
drink—as well as to bathe. This is why birds need
to have fresh, unpolluted drinking water available
to them 365 days a year. If you are fortunate enough
to live near a river or lake or have a brook running
through your property, you can expect a large number of birds to visit your garden, especially on warm
days. If you have no natural source of water nearby,
you will need to provide your birds with some kind
of container with water. In a very short time, you
will find that this water source acts as a magnet,
drawing species you would not ordinarily see in
your garden. In addition, it is interesting to observe
birds while they are drinking. Pigeons and doves
suck up their water, much like a horse, while swallows and swifts scoop up water with their lower
mandible as they skim across the water's surface,
often with their wing-tips making contact with the
water. Most small and medium-sized birds scoop
up some water and then throw their heads back,
allowing the water to run down their throats. Incidentally, swallows and swifts generally bathe on
the wing. Sometimes they completely submerge
their heads in a superfast dive, and sometimes they
settle for a quick splash, wetting just their undersides and parts of their heads and wings.

As noted earlier, if you have no natural body of
water nearby, you can install a pond or birdbath.
Garden centers have a variety of birdbaths to
choose from. One piece of advice: Stick to a simple
model, sometimes easier said than done. Most birdbaths are aesthetically ugly and constructed in such
a way that they are hard to handle and difficult to
clean and/or to fill with fresh water, which should

be done every day. My preference is for simple fiberglass dishes that can be placed on a few stones on the ground or on a pedestal. There is no law against having more than one birdbath. You can make things easier—and cheaper—for yourself by using a good-sized shallow container, such as a plastic or metal garbage can lid, placed on a few stones, with rocks grouped around it and some rock plants growing in between. Inside such a lid you can place some flat stones so that the birds can stand on these when bathing or drinking. You will need to clean these stones regularly, however, with a steel brush. Algae growth and the like will cause these stones to become super slippery, no longer affording the birds a proper grip. Do not use detergents or any other harmful cleaning agents, which would pollute the water.

During freezing weather in the winter you should use a thermostatically controlled heater like those in aquariums. The wires need to be very well insulated since this is an outdoor installation. Rest the heater in a layer of fine gravel (again like that used in aquariums) so that the container is not damaged nor the birds burnt by it. To prevent birds from bathing during freezing temperatures, which they will still do if given the chance, it is strongly advised that you cover your container during the winter with a piece of fine chicken wire, which will allow only drinking. Many hardware stores and garden centers have special outdoor immersion heaters, which are excellent for using with a birdbath. Just be sure to choose a model that has been designed to operate at a depth of $1-1\frac{1}{2}$ to $3-3\frac{1}{2}$ inches ($2\frac{1}{2}$–4 to 7–8 cm). I do not recommend water containers that are deeper than $3\frac{1}{2}$ inches, to prevent accidents. The heating element must have an automatic thermostat, of course, so that it will shut off as soon as the water has reached 42°F (7°C). If you use an extension cord, make sure that it is a heavy duty one, equipped with a triple-pronged grounded plug. Do not, under any circumstances, use glycerine or antifreeze to prevent water from freezing, because these chemicals cause damage to the feathers, that can be disastrous to birds, particularly during the winter. If you dissolve grape sugar in the water, this will retard freezing for quite some time, and in the case of severe frost, you will end up with a sort of congealed mess that the birds can peck at—a sort of frozen yogurt for birds.

Birdbaths and Ponds

Water should be conveniently available for the birds but should not provide us with a major chore. Ponds that have high, steep sides or birdbaths made of smooth plastic are not only difficult to clean but dangerous for the birds, possibly drowning them as they take a drink or bath. The surface from which a bird takes a drink or bath should be low and rough, not high and slippery. If all we have is a pond with steep edges, or a slippery birdbath, we should place a few rough stones in it (see page 21). Any water container that does not have sloping sides should be rejected. There is no point in buying a birdbath deeper than 3 inches ($7\frac{1}{2}$ cm), and this depth should have a gradual incline. In ponds with high edges you can plant reeds, in pots if necessary. The birds will slide down these reeds to get a drink, much like firemen down a pole. There are even those who manage to take a bath of sorts in this manner.

It is important that a pond or birdbath be situated in such a way that the birds have a clear view of the surrounding area. Between being distracted and being wet, a bird does not need the danger of not noticing a prowling cat or other enemy until it is too late to escape. Ponds and birdbaths should be situated so that they are accessible for you and can be seen from the house. Having a faucet nearby or a hose that will reach your chosen location is a definite plus. Being able to clean and fill with a hose makes things a lot easier. Lugging heavy buckets of water is a job no one has, as yet, derived any pleasure from.

There are several ornamental styles of birdbaths available. If you can afford it, I would recommend one made from concrete, cement, or ceramic. My own preference is for one that stands on a pedestal of at least 3 feet (93 cm), with the actual bath meas-

Birds in the Garden

uring 24 to 36 inches (61–91.5 cm) in diameter. Keep in mind that a severe frost can easily crack a bath made of terra-cotta or ceramic, rendering it useless.

There are pond molds available on the market, which will not cost you an arm and a leg. They are easy to install, and if you add oxygenating plants and some fish, you will have added something truly lovely to your garden. This pond should have some very shallow areas where birds or other animals can safely stand.

You can build a pond yourself by using heavy duty (at least 1,000 gauge) polyethylene lining. You start by digging out a hole according to your own design, removing any sharp stones and jutting roots to avoid puncturing the lining. For safety's sake you may want to add a thick layer of newspapers, again to prevent puncturing. Next you drop the lining over the excavated area, allowing plenty of overlap because you will be placing 2 to 3 inches (5–7.5 cm) of soil on top of this, plants (possibly in pots), and the dry stone edging. Of course, you could con-

Making a pond with free-form PVC liner.

1. Dig a hole with 9-inch shelf for plants; and a side slope of 15° to 20°. Remove all sharp stones and roots, and line the interior with sand.
2. Stretch the liner over the hole. Anchor the edges with bricks and stones.
3. Fill the pond with water. The weight of the water will carry the liner into the hole and mold it to the contours. Most wrinkles will disappear as the pond fills.
4. Trim away surplus liner, leaving a 6-inch flap around the rim.
5. Create a nice border allowing stones, bricks or whatever paving you choose to overhang the edge by 2 inches for a finished appearance. Maintain the water level by occasional topping off.

Birds in the Garden

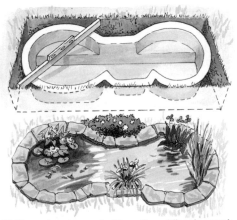

Making a charming pond with pre-formed liner is a much easier job.

The Dust Bath

Various birds, particularly sparrows and wrens, are very fond of a dust bath. This is how they keep their feathers in tip-top condition and rid themselves of parasites.

Fill an old metal or plastic garbage can lid with equal parts of soil, sand, and sieved ash. You may want to place this lid on a few stones to give it a steady base. A suitable location might be one that is somewhat sheltered, with a few bushes, low trees, and shrubs close by, but still sunny and facing south. If you want to do a thorough job, you might add a bug powder that is harmless to birds but effective against the pesky ecto-parasites that live on and between their feathers.

Trees and Shrubs for Backyard Birds

The trees and shrubs that make up a bird yard (and please remember to stick to native species, rather than foreign ones) must fulfill three functions:

1. shelter
2. nest sites
3. food

Obviously, not all trees and shrubs fulfill these requirements, but there are plenty of species that will (see page 23) and that will certainly not look out of place in your garden. So when you go to your local nursery, try not to pick only gorgeous, streamlined young trees and bushes. It won't hurt to pick a few that are less than perfect, symetrically speaking. These tend to offer more nesting locations, and we can always help this along by pruning. We can take a food shrub, one that is frequently visited by birds because of its berries, and convert it into a great place for shelter and breeding as well by some careful trimming and pruning.

First of all, let's take a look at a collection of the same plants that have formed a hedge. Beautiful

struct a pond of concrete, but be prepared for a major job. Such a pond needs to be at least 6 inches (15.5 cm) thick. Once the concrete is completely dry, it must be sealed with a coat of bituminous paint or waterseal cement. It is best to place a few inches of good aquarium soil on the bottom so that you can grow water plants in it. These plants need to be primarily oxygenating aquatic plants to help absorb the carbon dioxide that your fish and, after a while, various other uninvited guests such as newts, frogs, dragonflies and other insects produce. A few plants that are highly suitable for this purpose are: *Callitriche autumnalis* or starwort, *Eleocharis acicularis, Iris pseudacurus* or yellow flag, *Isoetes lacustris* or quillwort, *Polygonum amphibium* or *Amphibious bistort, Tillaea recurva*, and *Sagittaria graminea*. All these plants require a layer of soil of three to four inches in depth, and a water depth of 2½ to 5½ inches (6½–14 cm). A few snails (for example, *Planorbis corneus* or *Pauldina vivipara*) are a good idea because they remove algae from the sides of your pond, but not more than a few.

If you choose a heavy duty polyethylene-lined pond, you will, of course, need to place any water plants in pots in your pond so the roots don't push through the polyethylene.

Birds in the Garden

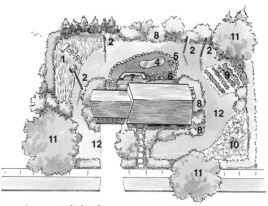

A suggested plan for an average yard.

1. Meadow plants	8. Shrubs (for food)
2. Bird houses	9. Vegetables
3. Herb garden	10. Nectar flowers for but-
4. Pond	terflies and humming-
5. Birdbath	birds
6. Bird feeders	11. Trees
7. Deck	12. Lawn

hedges can be achieved with privet, holly, beech, yew, and hawthorn. Such a hedge can serve as a divider bordering a neighbor's garden, or it can separate one part of your garden from another, such as your vegetable garden. A hedge needs to be fairly dense, so that it offers safe shelter. By removing some of the central stems, leaving forks, we are creating ideal nesting places. Of course, if a hedge is clipped too closely and grows too dense, it will no longer allow easy access to the birds. A hedge should be somewhat narrower at the top than at the bottom, the reverse of what usually happens. The top side can be trimmed in pyramid fashion, rounded, or flat. There are two important reasons to keep the base broader.

First, this allows more light to reach the lower leaves, keeping the lower regions of the hedge full with leaves. Second, this way a heavy snow-fall won't make the hedge top heavy.

While electric hedge clippers will work fine on privets and other small-leaf hedges, manual clippers will work better on larger leaf species like oak and beech. Even though you may feel that you have an excellent eye, it is wise to stretch a piece of thread along the top so that you will end up with a nice straight line rather than a bumpy one. Be sure to remove all cuttings from the hedge. If the hedge borders a street, of course you will want to sweep up all the cuttings together and remove them.

The best time for clipping most hedges is in the early spring and again after the summer. Do not do any pruning and trimming during the summer when the breeding season is in full swing.

As already mentioned, you do not want to seal the hedge so that the birds can't get in and out! A truely dense hedge will result only if you prune frequently. This is why we suggest pruning just twice a year. If your hedge does become too thick, you will need to thin it out. Incidentally, some shrubs, like the pyracantha and cotoneasters, require a regular cutting back in order to create a denser growth. If we keep to these guidelines, we will end up with hedges that provide beautiful facilities for nesting and shelter against the rain and wind. Such places are also used as sleeping quarters.

Dense shrubs offer the same opportunities, so it pays to keep in mind that new shrubs should be given locations not prone to strong winds. Birds will roost for many hours during the winter months, sometimes up to sixteen hours a day. It stands to reason that open bushes exposed to cold winds do not serve our purposes very well. Good shrubs, meaning those that provide shelter and nesting opportunities, are holly, laurel, and yew (this last one is also excellent as a hedge), and we haven't even considered the berries that are so much enjoyed by such a large number of birds. You can do something positive in retarding cold, northerly winds by placing several beech trees behind the bushes mentioned earlier, because the beech trees retain their leaves during the winter and offer an excellent windbreak. Open trees and shrubs can be improved by allowing ivy to grow over them. Ivy also offers great shelter and nesting places.

Keep in mind when planting a new garden those

Birds in the Garden

species that will bear berries and fruit or attract insects. Oak is a good insect-attracting tree, but it takes a long time before a young tree finally becomes of more use to birds. If you already have one or more oaks in your garden, take care of them, because an oak is a habitat in itself.

Species that grow faster and also attract insects are willows and live birches. Don't forget the possibility of an apple or pear tree, which offers insects and spiders excellent shelter with its rough bark. Many birds will enthusiastically seek these insects out. Allow a few apples or pears to remain on the tree after you have harvested the crop—they offer our winged friends a rare treat. The trunk and thicker branches often have holes that make great nesting places for treecreepers, nuthatches, and, obviously, various woodpeckers. Poplars offer places for a diversity of thrushes that will wake you each morning with a vibrant concert delivered from the highest branches. What more could a person ask for?

Unless you find it objectionable, don't get rid of a dead tree immediately. By simply leaving it alone for a few years, you will create your own little ecosystem. Insects and spiders will be found in and about the decay as the tree decomposes, providing food for many birds. The same principle is involved when we recommend that you do not get rid of a capped treetrunk. Here again, this is a warehouse of snacks for birds, there for the taking. If such a trunk is unsightly to you, plant some clematis next to it, and you will soon have a lovely piece of nature to enjoy.

Berry-bearing Trees and Shrubs

Barberry (*Berberis darwinii, B. vulgaris*, etc.)

Excellent nestsides for thrushes, finches, etc. The red berries are high in vitamin C and are a favorite with many different birds. The large thorns allow this plant to serve as an excellent hedge.

Blackberry (*Rubus fruticosus*)

This well-known plant, also called a bramble, attracts many bird species. Robins love the berries, as do blue jays, blackbirds, thrushes, thrashers, titmice, waxwings, bluebirds, evening grosbeaks, catbirds, cardinals, mockingbirds, towhees, and many others. Many species will also build their nest here, particularly if you maintain some good dense bushes.

Cotoneaster (*Cotoneaster horizontalis, C. buxifola, C. simonsii, C. dammeri, C. watereri, C. prostata,* etc.)

The big advantage of these plants is that they bear their fruit late in the year. They are favored by finches, thrushes, waxwings, and blackbirds. *C. simonsii* makes a good hedge; *C. buxifola* is excellent as an evergreen wall-climber.

Crabapple (*Malus* spp.)

Many finches like to build their nests in the crabapple, while waxwings and thrushes, among other species, enjoy the fruit.

Elderberry (*Sambucus nigra*)

Titmice, starlings, sparrows, cardinals, flickers, mockingbirds, chickadees, goldfinches, robins, towhees, wrens, waxwings, house finches, bluebirds, and thrushes are but a few of the many species that are very fond of this plant, to put it mildly. They like to build their nests in it and seek shelter from cold, snow, and rain, and of course they love to snack on the purple berries. It is a fast grower as well, and so offers all kinds of opportunities.

Firethorn (*Pyracantha* spp.)

There are very few birds that do not enjoy this plant. It is best to plant firethorn against the wall of your house or garage, training it up the sides. Many thrushes not only enjoy the berries but use the shrub for a nesting location. Flycatchers also often choose this plant as the site for their future nursery.

Hawthorn (*Crataegus monogyna*)

Robins, blue jays, brown thrashers, cedar waxwings, Eastern bluebirds, Eastern phoebe, evening grosbeaks, cardinals, finches, mockingbirds, and many more enjoy the dark red haws in early

24

Birds in the Garden

winter. This plant can also serve as an excellent hedge.

Holly (*Ilex aquifolium*)

When holly hedges become too thick and dense, they are no longer easily accessible to the birds. Clever pruning and trimming can prevent this from occurring. It is important to know that if you want to have berries, you should choose primarily female plants. Thrushes, finches, doves, and starlings are crazy about the berries, as well as many other species!

Honeysuckle (*Lonicera* spp.)

This plant is a fantastic climber. With regular pruning you will create a densely leafed plant and, consequently, many ideal shelters. The flowers attract insects, and the berries are gleefully consumed by many bird species, including goldfinches, robins, thrushes, cedar waxwings, bluebirds, evening grosbeaks, cardinals, mockingbirds, purple finches, and white-throated sparrows. The Japanese honeysuckle (*L. japonica*), being an evergreen, provides good shelter year-round.

Ivy (*Hedera helix*)

When ivy is exposed to plenty of light, it will bloom profusely with little white flowers, which attract many insects and, therefore, many birds. Allowing ivy to grow around trees certainly will not harm them, although the opposite is often declared. It is best not to plant ivy against a brick wall because the small roots can do serious damage to the mortar.

Privet (*Ligustrum vulgare*)

You can achieve an excellent privet hedge by trimming small amounts twice a year (see page 23). Don't forget some inside trimming too, to create a good selection of nesting forks. Remember that the black berries are poisonous for humans.

Rowan or mountain ash (*Sorbus aucuparia*)

This plant is a must in every bird garden. Its red berries are particularly appreciated by many birds.

Wayfaring tree (*Viburnum lantana*)

The red berries are treasured by robins, waxwings, bluebirds, thrushes, cardinals, finches, mockingbirds, and many others. The same can be

Trees carry fruits and seeds, many of which are enjoyed by birds. From left to right: Top: ash, maple, and pine. Middle: beech, holly, and red alder. Bottom: elm, pin cherry, white oak, and balsam poplar.

said for the guelder rose (*V. opulus*), which is very attractive with its clusters of red berries.

Yew (*Taxus baccata*)

I saw a lot of this slow growing evergreen in England, both as a tree, growing as high as 9 feet (3 m) and as high hedges, as dense as 6 feet (2 m), in churchyards. The story goes that yews were purposely planted to prevent the local peasants from allowing their livestock to graze in the churchyard. So much for charity! The foliage and bark are poisonous, and the seeds are toxic as well. Many thrushes, however, enjoy the pink berries, whose seeds leave the bird's body intact. It may take 12 years or more before the yew bears berries. It does, however, provide excellent nesting and shelter places.

A Few Other Trees Suitable for a Bird Garden

• **Alder**: Warblers like to look for insects in the alder tree, and finches are in heaven picking the seeds out of the small cones.

• **Ash**: Pine grosbeaks like to spend time in this tree, enjoying the ash-keys.

Birds in the Garden

• **Beech**: In the fall the nuts are happily consumed by all kinds of finches, chickadees, nuthatches, and woodpeckers.

• **Oak**: The oak provides a varied food source for countless bird species, with its rich insect and spider communities. The acorns are a favorite with pigeons and blue jays.

• **Poplars**: This tree is also a vast insect and spider warehouse. Redpolls like to feed on the catkins in the spring.

Flowers and Weeds for Birds

Many flowers have seeds that are nutritious for the birds, and their outstanding colors and shapes make them an asset for any bird garden. Take as an example the sunflower, which is especially appealing to the finch species. It is fascinating to watch the antics of finches as they attempt to obtain the seeds held captive by the sunflower. Nuthatches and titmice also like to feast on sunflowers. Other flowers that have much to recommend them are the China star, cosmos, scabious, evening primrose, phlox, and antirrhinum.

There are also plants that attract all sorts of insects, including the beautiful butterflies. The following feed plants come to mind: Michaelmas daisies, buddleia, ice plant, and veronica. Forget-me-nots are used by the beak-full as nesting material by many finches which all the while enjoy the seeds as well.

If you are the owner of a large garden, you might seriously consider allowing a small part of it to revert to a piece of wild nature, hopefully without provoking the wrath of your neighbors. This would allow some weeds to grow. The following plants are particularly useful in attracting insects, while offering the birds nutritious, edible seeds: dock, thistle, poppy, plantain, ragwort, knapweed, teasel, corn flower, groundsel, nettles, hebe, petunia, thyme, sweet rocket, godetia, lobelia, balsam, aubretia, lavender, night-scented stock, and valerian.

Excellent shrubs and plants are, from left to right: Top: ivy, elder, and mountain-ash berries. Bottom: American bird berry, hawthorn, and privet.

Here again it will be primarily finch species that are attracted to these plants.

Controlling Unwanted Weeds, Pests, and Predators in the Garden

Unfortunately, there are several products on the market that pose a dangerous threat to our environment and this includes our health. As far as I am concerned, organochlorine insecticides should be taken off the market, and their use totally forbidden, with heavy penalties imposed on those peo-

Above left: The least flycatcher is the noisiest of all flycatchers, especially during spring and early summer.
Above right: The eastern phoebe, also a flycatcher, says its name repeatedly.
Below left: The tree swallow's food includes, besides insects, berries and seeds in the cold weather.
Below right: The black-billed magpie behaves in a very shy manner on its rare visits to feeding stations.

Birds in the Garden

Some wild flowers for your backyard, from left to right: Top: rape seed, valerian, and teasel. Middle: hemp nettle and lesser snapdragon. Bottom: wild rosehip and forget-me-not.

ple who want to use up these harmful products rather than waste them. Fortunately, current trends show the public's collective consciousness, as well as conscience, being raised, albeit slowly, and we have come a certain distance from, say, the 1960s, when people brought about the death of thousands of birds with toxic chemicals on farmland and gardens. We need only to think back to the many birds of prey and water fowl that died during that period or that laid eggs incapable of being hatched. The plummeting population of the osprey is but one re-

Above left: The black-capped chickadee breeds often in a decayed pine or birch stump.
Above right: The tufted titmouse nests in tree cavities, old woodpecker holes, or bird boxes.
Below left: The red-breasted nuthatch prefers sunflower seeds, suet, and peanut butter.
Below right: The brown creeper likes suet but is largely insectivorous.

sult of a food chain disrupted by the use of chemicals, in this case DDT.

We can generally assume that other herbicidal chemicals used to control weeds are not dangerous for people and aninmals, but there are benefits in allowing some weeds to grow. They provide an excellent food source for many birds.

If you have definite reasons why you feel it is necessary to use chemical preparations, please adhere to the following guidelines:

• Carefully study the label and directions, including those on the enclosed instruction leaflets. Never exceed the recommended dosage. If something is not clear to you, contact the manufacturer or ask for further information at the garden center where you purchased the product.

• Be careful to avoid any spillage while mixing chemicals.

• Never spray on windy days, so the chemicals will not land in areas where they are not needed and may do more harm than good.

• If you spray anywhere near water sources, it is essential that you take care never to pollute the water, another reason not to spray on windy days.

• The above point of course precludes us from cleaning our spray equipment in natural water sources.

• Tightly seal any leftover chemicals and store them in a safe place, not accessible to children or pets, preferably in a locked cabinet. Be sure that the label and directions remain clearly legible, so that when the chemical is used again, there will be no question as to what it is and how to use it. Sometimes colored labels on chemicals become stained, making the label very difficult to read. If this is the case with one of your containers, put on a new label or make notations so that the identification and instructions remain clear.

• Used containers should be discarded in accordance with existing regulations. The label will generally state the method of disposal. If not, wrap the container in newspapers and put it in the garbage. Never leave empty containers lying around.

Birds in the Garden

Squirrels, raccoons, and rats, to name just a few mammals, will try everything to get to a bird feeder. To prevent this place "baffles" around the tree trunks or poles on which the feeders are mounted.

• Spraying equipment should be kept in excellent condition.

• Unless the instructions specifically say that it is permissible, never mix different chemicals in a container. If you use one container for more than one chemical, then of course you must clean the container before switching to another chemical.

Weeds: If you wish to eliminate weeds in your garden, you have four choices, all of which are extensively covered in various garden books:

1. fertilization
2. cultivation
3. mulching
4. biological control

The manager of your favorite garden center will undoubtedly be able to be of service to you in this regard.

Slugs: There are jugs and trays on the market that contain the extremely dangerous chemicals *metaldehyde* and *nuthiocarb*. These containers must be dug into the ground and must be properly covered so that birds, housepets, and children cannot get near them. Diatomaceous earth, which is completely safe, has also been found effective against slugs. Ask for advice on this subject at your garden center.

Insects. Many insects are an excellent part of a bird's diet. Some insects, however, are less suitable. Aphids (even though many tits like to eat them), flies, mealy bugs, and ants can be sprayed with soapy water, followed by clear water. Malathion or pyrethrum work very well also. If you have an infestation of one of these insects that has gone beyond control by these methods, you can use rotenone, which will also control flea beetles and Japanese beetles. Bean beetles and harlequin bugs are best combatted with pyrethrum.

Cats and Dogs: There are several commercial cat and dog repellents on the market that work effectively. Your own outdoor cats and dogs can be supplied with a bell attached to the collar, giving the birds some warning that danger lurks. Bird feeders should be placed so that they are not subjected to the unexpected leap of a cat on the prowl. Feeders, therefore, should be at least 15 to 18 feet (4.5–5.5 m) away from bushes, trees, hedges, low walls, etc.

Squirrels and Raccoons: I am hesitant to mention squirrels—I am very fond of them—but neither may I leave them out. It always gives me pleasure to watch their acrobatic antics, but I am the first to admit that, along with raccoons, they are a nuisance in a bird garden. We can prevent a lot of aggravation by elevating our bird feeders 5 to 8 feet (1.5–2.5 m) from the ground, and about 15 feet (4.5 m) away from trees, shrubs, water fountains, and other places that might provide our bushy-tailed friend (or foe) with a starting point for his fabulous jumps. Keep in mind that squirrels do not shy away from using branches or twigs that hang over our feeders. Even electric wires will do if they allow the squirrels to reach the goodies on display in our bird feeder. You can be certain that these smart little animals will do everything in their power to reach their goal—the food in the bird feeder.

Food for Birds

The Various Feeding Groups

According to their preferences, birds are divided into a number of food groups. The foodstuffs mentioned are those that make up the primary food of a given group, though there may be variations in the feeding patterns. For example, seed-eaters often give insects to their young, and insect-eaters may indulge in seeds during the winter season. Probably most of us are aware of the classical example of the chickadees, which eat primarily insects during the summer, but switch to a seed menu in the winter.

Meat-eaters: This group consists of those birds with a strong and curved beak, with which they tear their prey. The have excellent vision, so they can spot their prey from great distances, and a pair of strongly clawed feet with which they catch and hold their victims. Eagles soar at great heights, from which they spy their prey, which usually inhabit open terrain. Hawks have the ability to remain motionless in the air. They allow themselves to descend in short little drops. In the last phase they literally drop down on their victim. They also spy their prey from the tops of trees, in which case they attack from behind. Falcons chase their prey from behind and grab it while in the air. Buzzards allow themselves to drop onto their prey. Owls are mostly nocturnal and will surprise their prey in a silent, floating flight.

Fish-eaters: Numerous birds have fish for their main course. Their digestive systems are appropriately adapted to this food, which is often high in albumin and fat. The albatross and stormy petrel allow themselves to fall into the water from the air with a smack, startling the prey, which is now within easy reach of their beak. Pelicans and cormorants are equipped with a large, distensible, membranous pouch in which they can store the fish they catch, allowing them to accummulate quite a number in a short time. Penguins and grebes hunt fish under water, while herons trudge patiently along the water's edge in search of small fish or perhaps a little frog. Spoonbills filter the muddy water through their bill, harvesting small fish and various invertebrates. Seagulls are clever in catching the hapless fish that come to the surface.

Carrion-eaters: Vultures and marabous belong to this scavenger group, and it is a curious thing that both birds have bald heads. These birds circle high up in the air, surveying a large area below. Hawks, seagulls, and stormy petrels often partake of dead prey.

Seed-eaters: Most of the finch species belong to this group. They shell the seeds before they swallow them. Poultry also belongs in the seed-eating group, but swallow the seeds whole, just as doves do, and seek their seeds primarily on the ground. The group that first shells the seeds, picks them from the grasses and such.

Insect- and Other Invertebrate-eaters: An enormous number of species belongs to this group, although they seek their food in highly diverse types of vegetation. Birds that catch insects in the air generally have a beak that is broader at its base. Examples of this group are flycatchers and swallows. Woodpeckers drum up their food out of a tree, and have a powerfully developed skull and tongue. Nuthatches do the same thing, and chickadees look for their food in the bark of a tree. Starlings and larks find most of their food on the ground.

Fruit-eaters: Some large but also some very small birds make up this group, which includes cassowaries, emus, toucans, and tanagers. Some birds eat nuts and seeds as well as fruit and often offer insects to their young.

Pollen- and Nectar-eaters: For many birds in this group, pollen and nectar are secondary foods, and not necessarily the main fare. But the trademark of this group is that they visit flowers to extract pollen and nectar from them. Examples are lories, hummingbirds, and white eyes (*Zosteropidae*). We can see incredibly diverse beak shapes among the hummingbirds. They can be quite ordinary, strongly curved, or even three times the length of the skull. The tongue is also adapted to this manner of procuring food. Lories have a thick, fleshy tongue,

Food for Birds

pencil shaped at the front, and covered with papillae. Hummingbirds often have a partially hollow tongue, which is forked at the front.

Grass-eaters: The goose is a bird that can live almost entirely on a diet of grass. It may be unusual for a bird to be able to digest such rough cell matter. The rare kakapo from New Zealand also lives primarily on leaves and twigs. This bird chews on the twigs while leaving them on the tree.

Turnip-eaters: A small group of birds eat primarily turnips. Some quail, pheasants, cranes, and ducks use this food source.

What Is Food?

Food is a collection of matter that each organism needs for normal growth, reproduction, and development, and for protection against infection. Growth is the enlarging of the body and comes about through the multiplication of body cells. The largest growth takes place among birds that have not yet reached adulthood and continues until a specific standard has been met. During growth, a bird's plumage is also formed.

Food consists of a number of chemical components, such as albumin, fat, carbohydrates, vitamins, minerals and water. Living creatures all need food with roughly similar components. When different animals are compared, their body makeup is found to be very similar, chemically speaking. For example, when you compare a chicken, a mare, a sheep, a steer, and a pig, the percentage of water in their bodies ranges between 54 and 60 percent, of albumin between 15 and 21 percent, of fat 17 and 26 percent. The percentage of ash lies between 3.2 and 4.6 percent. As an animal becomes older, the water percentage drops off, while the fat percentage increases. Individual differences between animals of the same species are determined by the type and amount of food taken in, among other things.

Birds need a diet that consists of protein, albumin, fat, minerals, vitamins, and water. If the diet lacks one or more of these components, a deficiency symptom or disease will appear. This may happen within a week or two but could take much longer. These symptoms are more likely to show themselves quickly in growing birds than in adults. In most instances, a deficiency disease will have specific symptoms.

It is often quite difficult to determine how much an animal needs of a specific component. In practice, deficiency symptoms are often caused by the lack of a combination of diet components, which makes it even more difficult to determine the culprits. A lowered resistance also beckons infections. Foodstuffs that a bird cannot do without are called essential foodstuffs, and this distinction concerns those foodstuffs that the animal body must have in order to remain healthy and be capable of reproduction. It is these foodstuffs, then, collectively known as nutrients, that should be offered to the birds. It is not difficult to determine whether a particular foodstuff is absolutely essential, but it is difficult to determine how much of it is necessary. Factors such as the type of bird, activity level, and climate of the habitat all play a role. If a bird is about to enter an egg-laying phase, that too will affect its needs since now there is a new requirement—namely, the matter that makes up the eggs.

Some components can be stored in the bird's body on reserve. Other nutrients, however, must be taken in every day. If this does not happen, sooner or later one or more symptoms will appear.

Nutritional Requirements of Birds in the Wild

The availability of food in the wild has far-reaching consequences with regard to whether or not a bird species will remain in a particular region. The amount of food will be influenced by the season and climatic ranges, so throughout the year fluctuating amounts of seeds, fruits, insects, etc. will be present. It is an awesome and time consuming task to do research in the wild focused on determining an accurate image of exactly what and how much a bird eats. Such a study would include an examination of the crop as well as the stomach contents to see which nutrients are present, even though this would in no way shed any light on the availability of food in the wild. It would only tell us what the bird has recently consumed. We would need to examine a great many birds from a great many regions throughout an entire year to get any idea of the average. But the necessity to kill the birds being examined precludes this channel of research. If we study the immediate environment of a given bird, we can get an indication of the edible matter produced in that particular region. The best way to discover the staple of a bird's diet lies in close observation of the bird itself. Overall body build, shape, and type of beak are the best indicators.

We have seen that birds will sometimes eat insects and then switch to fruit or seeds, according to availability and need. When a bird cannot switch to a different food, a lack of the required food can force a drastic decision—namely, to move away. This is called migration, and the new habitat may be thousands of miles away.

Bird Feeders and Other Feeding Equipment

Before deciding where to place bird feeders, feedbells, and the vast array of other related equipment available on the market, we must observe the birds. Their safety and protection is at the top of our priority list. This also implies that our choice of equipment be determined by its usefulness for the birds, and not just by its ability to please us aesthetically. The chosen location—particularly during the winter—should protect the food from rain, wind, snow, and ice. The birds should have easy access to the food, and not fall an easy prey to cats, nor be overrun by sparrows and starlings.

These are only the most common nuisances that come to mind (see also page 30).

A well-constructed bird feeder also has the advantage of not costing an arm and a leg. Although we don't normally begin with the negatives, I will mention a few here simply to help you avoid some of the more common mistakes.

• The location must never be on a window sill or ledge.

• Don't construct a little feeding house through which the wind can blow, scattering the food, and into which the rain can reach, wetting the food and making it useless.

• Don't ever feed the birds strongly seasoned or salty meat or sausage scraps.

An important motto is: Feed regularly and at the same times.

Now that we have covered the above important points, we can take our hands out of our pockets and get started with the actual building. If you have little time for puttering around, you can limit yourself to hanging up a few feedbells. There are several models available in seed and feed stores, as well as in nurseries and pet shops. They are simple enough to make: Hammer a small nail with a large head through one end of a pencil or a wooden dowel. Place the pencil through the hole at the bottom of a fairly small flowerpot, so that the pot will hang from the nail. The pencil should not stick out of the top of the pot by more than 3 inches (7.5 cm). You can use a tin can or half of a coconut instead of a flowerpot if you prefer. Hang this feeder from any sturdy branch.

Apart from the feedbell, you can quite easily make feeder sticks. During the fall, look for a couple of sunflower stalks. Choose the thickest ones you can find, and cut them into pieces of about 12 to 20 inches (30–50 cm). Carefully cut each piece lengthwise along one side with a knife, removing about one-third of the stalk. Take out the pulp inside the stalk, leaving about 1¼ inches (3 cm) at each end, resulting in a long, narrow feeding trough. A notch cut at each end will serve as a place to tie a string or wire with which to hang or attach our

Food for Birds

creation. If sunflower stalks are not easily available, you can use a piece of bamboo, working it in the same manner, but using the natural "knots" as the ends.

Even those who own few tools and have been cursed with two left hands can safely attempt the construction of a canopied feeder. The most useful canopied feeder would be about 14 inches long (35 cm) and 2 to 2½ inches high (5–6 cm). The flat roof is 2¾ to 3½ inches (7–10 cm) wide. Two perches, about 14 inches (35 cm) long, ¾ inch (1.5 cm) wide, and ¼ inch (.5 cm) thick, are attached along the bottom edges of the side walls. About half way up on the inside we attach other thin strips of wood, to help hold on to the food. The side walls are about ½ inch (1 cm) thick. The inside surfaces should be as rough as possible. We can hang up the canopied feeder with wire threaded through two small screw eyes attached to the side walls.

This type of feeder is used primarily by those bird species that are good climbers and can hang onto things upside down. This means that they are safe from sparrows and the food is not accessible to unwanted guests like mice and jays.

What kind of feed do you use in this type of equipment? Hemp, sunflower seeds, mawseed, oats, and beef fat. On a low flame, just high enough to melt the fat, mix the seeds, deciding on the ratio yourself. Don't use too much fat. In a heavy frost it becomes so hard that the birds can no longer pick the seeds out. If you use an insufficient amount, the seeds will simply fall out. While this concoction is still warm, spoon it into the feeders. Later on these feeders will prove to be the best places to get photographs (see page 11), but they do have one disadvantage: If the feeders are hung to enjoy the early spring sunshine, the fat softens and the food tends to drop out rather easily. If you live in an apartment building one or more floors up, be careful that the food does not fall down onto someone passing by underneath. Placing a few spruce branches above the feeders, thereby providing some shade, prevents this melting and falling out business.

If you would like to observe and photograph

A diagram showing the assembly of a bird table/feeder. (See also illustrations on pages 35 and 36.)

birds besides the climbing varieties, here are a few additional pointers about feeders. For starters, you can use a feeder with a window—the size of which can vary depending upon the width of the designated window. The side walls should be fastened to the floor with rust-proof screws. The back of the feeder is open up to the support beam. The window at the front of the feeder is kept in place with grooves at the sides and bottom.

If you have a permanent spot available for a bird feeder, it is possible to choose a bird feeder house. This should be placed not too far from bushes and trees so that our little guests can escape quickly in the event that some uninvited guests should appear, like cats or sparrow hawks. This permanent bird feeder house can be used to observe the birds in their breeding cycles during the spring if you install a few nesting boxes at that time. The one-time, somewhat larger expense in the initial construction—for sturdier wood for the frame and roof, asphalt paper, and glass for the window—is well worth it. In the window feeders as well as in the bird feeder house, place oil-containing seeds, such as hemp, sunflower seeds, mawseed, halved seeds from melons, linseeds, beechnuts, and broken pieces of peanuts for the scramblers among them.

Food for Birds

For the true seed-eaters, we can add some oats, white millet and canary grass seed. The insect-eaters get rolled oats, raisins, apple pits, pear pits, and sorb apples, haws, elderberries, as well as overripe fruit from the house.

For birds that seek most of their food on the ground, you can build a feeder especially adapted for them. You need only a few pieces of wood laths, some wire, some branches to cover it all, and a sturdy wire mesh around the structure to protect the birds from cats.

The Arrival of the First Guests

These various structures are necessary for the later observation of birds. However, don't become impatient if your newly constructed feeder is not immediately overrun with visitors. The birds need to find it first. You can hurry this discovery along by placing a few store-bought feederbells or the like in close proximity to your structure. However, the time it takes before the birds have located and accepted your new feeding place is usually dependent upon flight patterns that lead to your house. For example, a large park somewhere in the neighborhood and trees in rows along streets leading to your house would establish a flight pattern. Even if you are located on a street that has no trees or bushes, fear not. It will just take a little longer before the birds discover your new restaurant.

When we wait for something, we usually pay close attention to the details of our surroundings. We tell our family members to be on the lookout for any birds in the area. In any event, it will not be long before there is a buzzing, hopping, jumping, and fluttering from tree to tree in your street. Chickadees, tree creepers, and nuthatches, normally neatly divided into their own breeding territories, have found themselves in a migration organization and are wandering through the neighborhood. This organization seems to have adopted a clearly visible

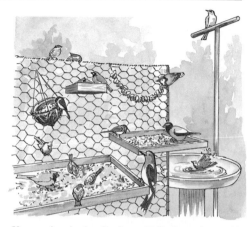

Use your imagination. Feeders, a birdbath, perches—with such a set-up it shouldn't take long to attract bird visitors.

flag, because, like a flying pennant, a woodpecker is in the lead. As is the case with the other birds, the woodpecker's wandering instincts have been awakened and lured him far away from his traditional woods. And so a new feeding place is discovered. A few chickadees desert the wandering group and choose our feeder for their midday meal. Apart from the house sparrows, the chickadees are usually the first and later the most loyal of our visitors. They perform like artists on the flying trapeze, with their wonderful acrobatics, and are the core of the daily program on view from our window.

Not very timid, and in constant motion, the chickadees clamber about on the feeder. They deftly loosen a sunflower seed and fly away with it to the nearest tree, where they open the shell. Slowly but surely the rumor makes the rounds—there is a new food source over at your house. More and more birds appear, and soon your feeder area looks like Grand Central Station. If you are a close observer, you will see that not only does each species differ from another, but each individual bird has its own personal characteristics as well. In just a little while, you will recognize the aggressive ones that try to push the others aside. And you will know the timid individuals, looking over the whole scene each time from a safe distance before venturing out into all the excitement going on at the feeder. You will recognize the forming of an overall feeding and behavior pattern out there on your window sill. Grab a notebook and start taking some notes. They will come in handy later on when you start taking some photographs.

On a certain day, one of the chickadees that frequented my window began to let himself be heard. He drummed away at the putty that held the window in place. In a very short time he was no longer drumming alone but had been joined by three other chickadees. This business had now gone beyond being amusing, and I had to consider what might be done about it. Then it suddenly occurred to me that this window had just been replaced a few days ago. The glazier had used linseed oil in preparing the putty, and because the weather was so very cold, had been rather heavy handed with it. It was the linseed oil that had prompted the chickadees to cheerfully peck away at the putty, which amazed me since I felt I had offered them far better food.

This type of communication among chickadees has been public knowledge for some time among English housewives. In England, milk is delivered in bottles, placed at front doors each morning. A few chickadees discovered these bottles during their wanderings and pecked at the lids. Since they were very pleased with the rich cream that lay at the top, they made a regular practice of opening the bottles. It started in a certain part of the city, and then the practice broadened in ever-widening circles. It came to the attention of a few English bird enthusiasts, who started to take notice of this behavior. It appeared that the chickadees, in a kind of self-training effort, concentrated themselves on specializing in the opening of these bottles and moved from one part of the city to another. As reported later, this attack on the milk bottles became so widespread that the dairies had to switch to a new kind of lid, impenetrable to the pecking of birds.

Feeding Birds Around the House and Garden

Pet shops, supermarkets, and even many nurseries carry a large variety of wild bird seed from sunflower seeds, unroasted unshelled peanuts, suet bells, and universal food, to corn and hazelnuts. The peanuts can be threaded on a thin cord with a strong needle. With this food, you will be helping a number of birds that come by your home. Mixed seed for outdoor birds is enjoyed by all seed-eaters. There are birds, however, who look for their food only on the ground, while others restrict their food hunting to bushes and trees. This is why finches are often rather timid about getting their food on feeding platforms. They normally find their food on the ground. The white crowned sparrow will also be

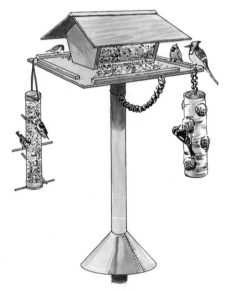

An excellent, covered bird table, placed on a slippery pole, and with a metal cone for extra protection. Left, a commercial tube feeder for thistle/niger seed. Right, a log feeder with suet.

Food for Birds

seen under the feeding table, looking for spilled seeds. Chickadees, house sparrows, starlings, hairy woodpeckers, and sometimes mourning, common ground, and wood pigeons are more frequent visitors to the feeding platform. Nevertheless, even the ground varieties will lose some of their shyness when the weather becomes cold enough. The thrush types can then be found both on and under the feeders.

We do not recommend margarine, because it causes diarrhea, but a cheap, saltless, fairly hard plant fat can be hung up in feeding-hives. Apart from the chickadee varieties, this will also attract finches, sparrows, blackbirds, nuthatches, hairy woodpeckers, and even kinglets, tufted titmice, and, of course, starlings.

Mashed apple and pear peels, and even the seed housing will be eaten by thrushes, in limited quantities. Overripe apples are a great food source, and we may be able to pick up a number of them for little or no money at the local farmstand or in the vegetable department at the supermarket. Coconuts are an old-fashioned bird food. These can be served either by cutting them in half or by cutting a feeder hole in the shell. Within no time, the entire coconut will be eaten clean.

It should be pointed out that tufted titmice in particular are crazy about little pieces of white bread. Northern mockingbirds, blue jays, and hairy woodpeckers know what to do with hazelnuts. The woodpeckers bring the hazelnuts someplace where they can clamp them and chop them up. Nuthatches and chickadees do something similar with sunflower seeds. They can be seen flying to and fro with their precious cargo. Red-winged blackbirds and sparrows, on the other hand, may spend a great deal of time at the feeder tables. The house wren can be best fed with universal food, placed in the nooks and crannies of the trees they frequent. Brown creepers may take advantage of that food source as well.

We can feed bread to the birds, but it should be cut into small pieces so that the birds do not end up taking large pieces back to bushes and trees, and

A fruit skewer for fruit and nectar loving birds is easy to construct.

generally losing them there. Birds that later find these pieces of lost bread are an easy target for cats and other predators. So be sure that the pieces are not so big that birds fly away with them. If you would like to somewhat discourage the impertinent house sparrows, you can run some black thread around feeders that have a roof. Tumblers and various finches will crawl right through the threads, but sparrows do not dare.

Grain wastes, oats, millet, and crushed peanuts are also all enjoyed by many species. Kitchen wastes are a tricky thing. Never throw out more than is immediately eaten, because it becomes a mess, spoils very quickly, and is sure to attract rats. Feeding places on the ground should be picked with care. Birds need to have a clear view of their surroundings so that they have enough time to get away, if necessary. Here again, the food should not be left for any length of time. When snow is expected, you can use an old piece of carpet or a large piece of plastic and lay it down at a feeding spot, holding it in place with a few stones at the corners. This will keep the feeding spot clear of snow. Old newspapers will do as well, but be sure they don't blow away—your neighbors might get a little testy. Small garden ponds can be kept from freezing, for a while anyway, by covering them when severe frost is expected, or perhaps overnight, with a few pieces of wood. These can be removed again during the day. Do not put out water during heavy frost, and during freezing temperatures put out water only for drinking, not for bathing. A saucer with a cup turned upside down in the center fulfills this need nicely. Or you can stretch some fine wire across a water dish to achieve the same result. White ceramic dishes are not a good choice because they are very slippery and the color is too stark, scaring the birds away. A far better choice is a rough and dark earthenware dish, nice and heavy so it will not tip over very easily. When it snows, the birds do not need you to provide them with water since they can take in their moisture needs from the snow. Do not add glycerine or salt to their water. A spoonful of sugar is all right and will lower the freezing point of the water.

Some people place a dish of water on an upside

Feeders for small birds. A bird feeder with wire mesh (top) is an excellent solution in case you have many large birds in your backyard. The mesh allows small birds to get to the food easily, but keeps the larger species out. The globe feeder (left) can only be used by small birds. The plastic seed hopper (right) is especially appropriate for offering nuts and seed mixtures to small finches, siskins, and the like.

down clay flower pot and place a candle underneath. This is somewhat hazardous and if it falls over, could scorch a bird's feathers.

Winter Feeding

Why Feed Birds in the Winter?

The winter months are a difficult time for many bird species, both those that stay year-round and those that come to our area from more northerly regions. When the days are short and food is hard to come by, they still need to find sufficient amounts. When temperatures drop, a bird needs additional fuel to keep up his body temperature (fairly high at 104°F or 40°C), which puts an additional strain on food supplies. Many birds become weakened during the winter when not enough food

Commercial hummingbird feeders.

Food for Birds

Various suet holders. Suet, the fat trimming from meat, can be combined with various seeds or peanut butter and formed into small cakes (the so-called seed cakes). These treats provide a quick energy source.

is available. The winter months take their toll and only the strongest survive to multiply again in the spring.

Birds must devote the greater part of the daylight hours to foraging for food. With all this effort expended to obtain food, they need some rest periods in between, and each time they are disturbed, more energy and time are lost. Disturbing large groups of foraging ducks or geese in the winter can have a detrimental effect on their overall condition.

To get back to this section's question, in the first place we feed birds in the winter in order to help them get through it. But we can help only a relatively small number of different species. Winter feeding is full of good intentions, but nowadays it is less important for many species than in the past. The birds that profit most from such feeding are the very ones that generally survive best anyway, such as starlings, blue jays, cardinals, mourning doves, tits, and chickadees. Nevertheless, the educational aspects of feeding birds are still considered impor-

tant. It brings man closer to nature and to birds in particular. It is a great learning experience for children, and promotes general awareness of the need for bird protection.

Winter feeding around the house starts to pay off when ice storms, sleet, or snow cut off the sparse food available for the birds. During long and severe winters, many birds have an extremely difficult time. And when winter is late in coming, many birds tend to hang around, hardly considering it necessary to travel further south, duped by the milder temperatures, only to find that February comes with unexpected fury.

Birds out in the field are more difficult to help. Water birds concentrate on bodies of water that do not freeze over quickly or look for holes in the ice. Once everything is frozen solid, the strong have left, and the weak are left behind on the ice, sometimes frozen to it.

Then everyone jumps into action—bird protection agencies, bird work groups, bird sanctuaries, even police, military personnel, school kids, and homemakers. Food is brought to difficult-to-reach areas, sometimes even via helicopter. School children gather bread, abattoirs offer leftover wastes, as do fishmongers, grain dealers, and food preparation plants. Many bird sanctuaries and zoos are suddenly overwhelmed with all kinds of winter victims. The press, radio, and television usually make their announcements when the damage has already been done, but they forget to warn that many more victims are out there among the hungering ducks, gulls, finch and thrush species that look for their food elsewhere. Organizing help from one central point per county would be far more effective.

When Should We Feed Birds During the Winter?

The time to feed them is when things start to get tough. You could try to start putting some food varieties out around December (see page 38). Start with small quantities, and make adjustments as necessary. Be sure that nothing is left lying around. It

Food for Birds

attracts mice and rats, and spoils. Any food you put out should be totally consumed well before dark each day. Food that contains a lot of moisture, such as overripe apples, freezes quite quickly and is then difficult to eat. Rotting food and bird droppings can carry infectious diseases. Salmonella bacteria can cause a particularly contagious paratyphus. In the spring, when birds are in their weakest state, they may contract this disease—usually fatal for them—because of unhygienic conditions at feeding tables established by people.

Out in the field, this illness is not so prevalent because it typically occurs where man has distributed food for the birds with a careless hand. Infected birds suffer severe diarrhea. In a flash, their droppings have spread this deadly disease to other birds, particularly seed-eating and ground-feeding varieties. This is why feeding bells, automatic feeders, and such are so much more hygienic than feeder tables, covered or not. No matter how good your intentions, don't overfeed, especially during the winter.

What should you feed the birds during the winter? To answer this question we need to distinguish the feeding done around the house and garden from feeding in the open field.

Feeding Birds During the Winter in the Open Field

Birds in the open field are difficult to help. We need to determine which species we want to feed, and exactly what type of food these birds need.

You will now be dealing with larger numbers than when feeding birds around the house. You will need to become organized. Animal or vegetable food sources will have to be arranged. The food will need to be picked up and placed in large dishes or sacks. It may need to be prepared, chopped up, cut up, or in some other way reduced in size. Storage becomes a problem too. A roster needs to be worked up of the volunteers involved, and the days and times each is available to go into the field. Pos-

sible food sources are: greens and fruit from farmstands or supermarket vegetable departments; fish refuse from fish markets and stores; meat wastes from abattoirs and meat packing plants; refuse from gristmills and other grain sources; leftovers from poultry slaughterhouses; stale bread supplied by bakeries or collected by youth organizations.

Paddle ducks seek their food in shallow water, and can eat both meat and vegetables, including chopped meat, greens, millet, mixed grains, corn, pigeon or chicken feed, bread mixed with some melted unsalted butter, shortening, or salad oil. Diving duck species are more difficult, because they take their food while diving through the water's surface. Good results have been achieved with finely cut potato peels or small pieces of raw potatoes that have been slightly frozen beforehand. When this food is sprinkled about in the water, it thaws and sinks very slowly toward the bottom. The merganser species as well as the grebe varieties can be helped with just meat and fish refuse. Don't forget that birds should always be given unsalted foods. Good results were obtained in Germany with underwater feeder floats. Wooden rafts 6 by 15 feet (2×5 m) had one side weighted down so that these floats drifted about $15\frac{3}{4}$ inches (40 cm) below the water's surface. In flowing waters these floats need to be anchored down, of course. Grain was fed from them. Barley appeared very suitable because it doesn't float easily; in addition, it contains 75 percent digestible foodstuffs, a high proportion. Geese can be helped with grain, sugarbeets, raw potatoes, and chopped greens. By plowing whole lanes on open fields with a snowplow on a tractor, grassy areas can be exposed for them.

Concentrations of herons and kingfishers are likely to be found by any bodies of water that have managed to remain unfrozen during severe frost. Be mindful of your eyes when around herons. They have been known to turn vicious. The herons' food preference is for refuse from poultry and meat packing plants, abattoirs, and fisheries. Kingfishers are more difficult to please. Feed them always at the same place, preferably when it is almost dark and

Food for Birds

the gulls have already settled down for the night. Feed them calmly, without a lot of fanfare, at a serene spot without a lot of wind, at the same time every day, and try to have the food brought by the same person. Heron types should be able to become accustomed to a situation like this. Refuse from poultry may be available in large quantities. Watch out that leftovers do not invite rats.

Although the winter feeding of owls requires the expertise of specialists, we do want to mention it here. In snow-free spots where owls might be seen during the winter, you can offer some help by providing meat refuse and live or dead mice. Animal victims of traffic accidents can also be used. Those who wish to feed owls need a good working knowledge of their behavior—but then, that rule really applies to the feeding of all species.

Apart from buying bird feed, you can gather food yourself for the winter months. You can gather seeds and berries, but it is a tricky job because you need to know the exact harvesting time for every plant, bush, or tree in which you are interested. Gathering berries from the mountain ash, hawthorn, rose-hip, blackberry, birdberry, ivy, privet, holly, cotoneaster, etc. needs to be done before the berries become overripe. Some people store the berries in containers, crates, or plastic tubs, alternating layers of dry sand with layers of berries. This seems to work well, but it is a good idea to experiment a little ahead of time, otherwise you may end up with moldy goods. Another way to preserve this food is by drying it in a low oven or over a wood stove. Only a large supply can help during the winter. It is also important to collect beechnuts, acorns, and chestnuts. Beechnuts are especially popular if you mash them. Acorns and chestnuts are often hidden in old nests or under shingles or under debris by blue jays. They sometimes do the same thing with hazelnuts.

The birds further appreciate seeds from trees and weeds. Birch seeds can be gathered by the bucketful, as can maple and elm seeds. Seeds from fallen berries from some yew species and from prunus species can occasionally be found during the winter. As far as weeds are concerned, there are the seeds of the dandelions, wild buckwheat, thistles, rapeweed, dockweed, and various grass seeds, not to mention the seeds of countless herbs. It will become clear to you soon enough which foods are the biggest favorites among the birds, so concentrate on those that are the easiest to gather and the most accepted. Just the gathering and collecting of food for the birds for the winter is a rewarding exercise.

Birds that live in the wild know which berries are potentially threatening to their health, and they also know which plants are pretty much entirely poisonous.

Caution Is the Watchword

- Never sprinkle food that contains salt (pork rind, bacon, peanuts).
- Don't feed large pieces that a bird may fly away with only to lose elsewhere. Don't feed food that can freeze, unless the pieces are large enough so that birds can peck smaller pieces from them.
- No salty cheese ends, which often have plastic or waxy protective coatings around them.
- Be sure that birds will not have the opportunity to bathe in their drinking water during freezing temperatures.
- Don't place spoiled fruit in orchards. It's not good for the birds, and the precaution can keep the fruit trees from becoming diseased.
- Don't throw the remains of seeds and gravel from cage birds outside for the outside birds, because you might unwittingly transmit a disease that way.
- Don't ever leave food for the birds too close to a street or traffic area.

Help With Nesting

The Nesting Season

It should not come as a surprise that a garden with the right trees and bushes, thereby providing food and nesting locations, can expect lots of bird visitors. As soon as the first spring days are upon us again, and the delicate greens push away the browns and grays of winter, some new bird friends are likely to appear on the scene. Some of the species that have spent the winter may move to other areas at this time, only to be replaced by others.

The spirit of spring is in the air. Birds are chasing each other. They are busy determining their territories (usually done by the males), and a few fast workers are already dragging around bits of straw and other nesting materials. Before you know it, you will hear the peeping of robins and blue jays among the branches.

Several males have already chosen their own specific song post—the top of a bush, a bare branch, a fence post, a TV antenna, or a spot on one of your gutters. During these concerts they keep a sharp eye out for any bird that might display a desire to enter their territory. They will chase any rival away all the while calling loudly, or place themselves in front of the intruder, puffing up their feathers to appear larger, in order to quelch any invasion. It is to be hoped, the intruder will then beat a retreat. It rarely comes to actual fighting. Physical contact generally takes place only if the nest with eggs or young is threatened.

Such singing by the males is not simply a communication of territorial rights but also an extremely important part of courtship ritual. It says to females, "Come pay me a visit and let's become acquainted." When the female enters the territory of a singing and invitation-extending male, he will do everything he can to respond to her interest with a display of a "threatening" nature. Females in the bird world are not easily intimidated, so she does not take flight but stays where she is, taking on a submissive posture with tucked-in head and fluffed-out feathers. And if she sticks to the thought that the one who maintains position the longest wins, she will be accepted by the male. In the event that two females are attracted by the enthusiastic song of a male and enter his territory, it is not the male who decides between them, but the females themselves who fight it out by aggressive display. There are numerous forms of courtship, and they all contribute to the highly interesting study that makes bird watching so fascinating.

After the courtship comes the building of the nest. The birds will search for suitable nesting locations, which really means that the male goes looking, but the female has the final say. And you, as birders, help this process along a little by providing the birds with several nesting boxes, which you have, of course, hung up several weeks in advance. Don't be too surprised if a bird couple chooses four or more locations, start with the nest building, only to stop suddenly a few days later and start somewhere else. Eventually the female will make her final decision, which will be evidenced by her lining the nest.

Competition for nesting sites often ends with the species you most wanted being driven away. Remember that each species has a right to make a nest, and if you have provided a suitable breeding opportunity, it would be silly to drive that species away. If you provide enough nesting boxes, which really means too many, then competition among the interested parties comes to a halt. On our one-acre property we have hung nine nesting boxes and two flower pots, and it is not unusual to have them all occupied.

Providing Nest Boxes

The majority of our garden guests can be divided into birds which either breed in hole nest boxes or prefer open-fronted nest boxes. Tits, for example, prefer hole nest boxes, while flycatchers and robins would rather raise a family in an open-fronted nest box.

Help With Nesting

Before investing in some wood and dragging out your hammer, some nails, and a saw from your workbench or tool shed, figure out what kind of birds you can expect to entice to your garden. If your knowledge of the various bird species is still limited, hang up just a couple of nest boxes of both varieties. No doubt they will soon be inhabited. It is a great feeling to know that there are couples in your garden that are breeding in *your* nest boxes. Take careful notice of the species that you encounter both in your garden and in the immediate surroundings during this first year. Next year you can add nesting boxes recommended for the particular species you desire to attract and have identified during the first year. This may well include species that prefer to build a free nest in a forked branch location. This might be high up in a tree, or somewhat closer to adult eye-level, or even quite low near the ground. Some species actually build their nests on the ground. But many will be very grateful for the nest boxes already mentioned. You may want to stick to the following rule: the diameter of the entrance hole of the nest box should not be too large—that is, if you want to prevent all your nest boxes from eventually being inhabited by only starlings and house sparrows. A diameter of 1⅛ inches (2.8 cm) will keep this from happening.

Materials

Nesting boxes made of synthetic materials are not recommended for the following reasons:

1. There is insufficient ventilation in spite of the fact that there may be openings along the top of the walls under the roof overhang.
2. They become loaded with static electricity, which attracts dirt particles that pollute the air and come through the opening.
3. The insufficient ventilation and insulation, as well as the high relative humidity, results in a climate within the nesting box that causes young birds to become sick, to die, and sometimes be born deformed.

Tests performed with nesting boxes made of artificial materials but constructed with wooden floors and roofs, as well as with ventilation openings under the roof along the top of the walls, did not produce better overall ventilation, nor an improvement in the absorption of moisture.

Synthetic boxes are admittedly maintenance-free, but good wooden boxes, when properly cared for, will last a long time.

Nesting boxes are made from all kinds of material besides wood—namely, cement, pvc, and stone.

Tips

- The material used to build the nesting box must be able to withstand the changing seasons, and provide sufficient thermal insulation. The thickness of the wood needs to be at least ½ inch (15 mm). Thinner wood will begin to crack and split very quickly. Besides providing a place in which to breed, nesting boxes are also used by many species as a shelter during the night for a good part of the year, especially during the winter.
- The nesting box should be watertight, even during heavy rain.
- The minimum living space should be 5 by 3½ inches (12 × 9 cm).
- The diameter of the opening determines the species that will make use of it.
- The interior should not be painted, so that the wood will be better able to absorb condensed moisture. The exterior should not be painted either, but certainly not with carbolinium. If you insist on painting it, use a good exterior stain at the most and do it months before the breeding season starts.

Life is much easier if nesting boxes can be cleaned simply. Never use insecticides.

- Clean them in February and in September or October. The interior walls should be smooth to facilitate cleaning.
- It is best to use hinges when installing the roof or to build the box so that the roof can be removed.
- The bottom should be removable as well.

Help With Nesting

It is important to prevent the accumulation of dirt and waste, to help prevent disease-carrying germs.

Construction

A basic birdhouse or nest box can be made as follows: Purchase a straight piece of wood about 5 feet (1.5 m) long, ½ inch (1.25 cm) thick, and 6 inches (15 cm) wide. Do not use soft woods, such as willow and poplar. I personally like cedar. Even though it is relatively soft, it is still practical and weathers excellently. Nest boxes made of pine or deal will do nicely too, and last a long time, provided they are treated with a preservative to prevent rot.

It is ideal if one of the sides of the wood is not milled smooth. You can use this on the inside of the nesting box, providing a good rough surface for the young to get a hold of when flying back into the

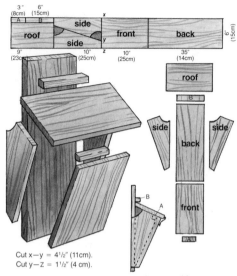

Cut x—y = 4½″ (11cm).
Cut y—z = 1½″ (4 cm).

Construction plan for wedge nest box, used by treecreepers and nuthatches.

nest. Cut the wood into the specific panels (see opposite). The entrance hole in the middle of the front panel—1½ inch (3.8 cm) in diameter—should be about 1 inch (2.5 cm) from the top. Do a neat and accurate job when drilling or sawing out this hole. To prevent water from entering the nest box, the roof panels should extend over the front of the box as well as over the sides. The edges of the entrance hole should be made smooth with a file and sandpaper. The same applies to every panel that you cut, so that the whole thing fits nicely when it is

Above left: The northern mockingbird often copies the song of other birds.
Above right: The population of the eastern bluebird has declined due to agricultural fungicides and pesticides.
Below left: When disturbed, the hermit thrush has a habit of raising its tail.
Below right: The striking cedar waxwings often room their habitats in flocks from ten to twelve to well over a hundred.

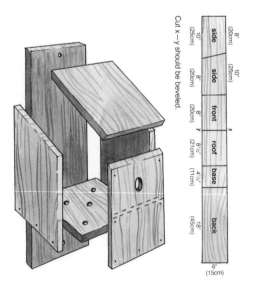

Plan for a basic hole nest box. Note the alternate for an open-fronted nest box, and the drainage holes in the bottom. Use a rubber, leather or metal hinge for the roof.

Help With Nesting

The wedge nest box on the left, with the entrance in the left top corner, as well as the strip of bark tacked to the trunk of a tree (right) are excellent nesting facilities for treecreepers and nuthatches.

ready to be put together. Never install a perch under the entrance hole because this makes it possible for squirrels, weasels, rats, and cats to get to the young and/or the eggs. In addition, sparrows sometimes take it upon themselves to park themselves on such a perch, annoying the rightful inhabitants, and making it difficult for them to fly in and out. Besides, who needs inquisitive glances when you are breeding or taking care of young-

Above left: The little ruby-crowned kinglet often flutters its wings—an excellent field mark!
Above right: The golden-crowned kinglet has a clear white stripe over its eye.
Center left: The red-eyed vireo is often called "preacher," due to its long "monologues."
Center right: The yellow-rumped or Myrtle warbler likes insects, sunflower seeds, berries, fruits, crumbs, and suet.
Below left: The yellow warbler has a musical voice.
Below right: The American redstart is the most animated of all the warblers.

sters? Don't forget to drill three or four drainage holes in the bottom, necessary for obvious reasons. It does not hurt, either, to drill perhaps three little holes in the side panels, assuring a certain ventilation. This comes in very handy when one of the parents or, later, one of the young birds decides to sit in the opening to view the outside world, blocking the fresh air flow. The roof panels must be adequately covered, as with asphalt paper. Once the box has been put together, it is ready to be hung up. Choosing a location at a height of 6½ to 16 feet (2–5 m). Against a tree trunk or wall would be the least risky spot.

The well-known birch blocks used for bird breeding by aviculturists in aviaries and cages are available at most nurseries. Various small tumbler species, and even wrens and warblers, like to use them. Be sure, however, that the entrance hole is no larger than ¾ to 1 inch (2–2.5 cm) in diameter.

Nest Boxes for Specific Birds

Although we show a number of different models of nest boxes in our illustrations, I would like to make a few comments on the specific boxes described below:

Treecreepers

Entrance hole: a crack measuring 1¼ by 4¾ inches (3 × 12 cm); nestbox: 4 by 5½ by 8¾ inches (10 × 14 × 22 cm).

This box is especially designed for treecreepers (see page 44). A vertical crack serves as entrance hole, and is located near the back on the side, next to the mounting slat. Nuthatches will also use this type of box. I have had a lot of success with nest boxes that had entrance openings at both sides.

Woodpeckers

For the small species, entrance hole: 2 inches (5 cm); nest box: 5½ by 5½ by 12 inches (14 × 14 × 30 cm).

47

Help With Nesting

For medium sized and large woodpeckers, entrance hole: 2½ inches (6.5 cm); nest box: 5½ by 6¾ by 19¾ inches (14 × 17 × 50 cm).

A hollowed-out, saucer-shaped block needs to be mounted at the bottom, to prevent the young from rolling out into the corners. Because a nest box for woodpeckers needs to be completely dark inside, allow the front side to extend 9 inches (23 cm). In addition, the thickness of the top half of the front panel is doubled by adding a second piece of wood. This makes the entrance hole more like a tunnel, which is, of course, the case in naturally occurring holes. Some birders stick to an entrance hole of 1¾ inches (4.4 cm), while medium and larger species are provided with a 2½ inch (6.5 cm) opening. This last dimension may invite screech owls to use the box as well.

Screech Owls

Entrance hole: 2¾ by 2¾ inches (7 × 7 cm); nest box: 19¾ by 19¾ by 11¾ inches (50 × 50 × 30 cm), or 10 by 12 by 12 inches (25 × 30.5 × 30.5 cm). This nest box has the inside space divided into two parts by an 8 by 8 inch (22 × 22 cm) insert. Very little light comes through to the actual breeding space in the back. Screech owls have become more dependent upon us than in the past because of the disappearance of many trees in the fields, as well as the clearing of orchards.

In the last few years, breeding pipes have come into vogue: the entrance hole is 2¾ inches (7 cm); the nest box is 6¼ by 6¼ by 27½ inches (16 × 16 × 70 cm), and sometimes as long as 38 inches (96½ cm). These breeding pipes can be round, oval, square, or triangular in shape, but should all have a diameter of about 6¼ inches (16 cm), and an entrance hole of 2¾ inches (7 cm). These boxes are affixed in a horizontal position to a branch, and in such a manner that overeager young cannot simply go wandering out onto the branches. The breeding pipe should be installed 6½ feet (2 m) above the ground. Prevent the rain from beating in by installing it so it doesn't face southwest.

A woodpecker/flicker nest box.

Barn Owls

Entrance hole: 8 by 8 inches (20 × 20 cm); nest box: 15¾ by 25½ by 15¾ inches (40 × 65 × 40 cm). The entrance hole is best located in one of the upper corners of the front panel. There are horizontal—29-inch (75 cm) long and 7¾-inch (45 cm) high—and vertical—7¾-inch (45 cm) long and 21¾-inch (55 cm) high—models available as standard sizes on the market. In England they use a box with the following dimensions: 35½ by 14¾ by 11¾ inches (90 × 37.5 × 30 cm). The unusual thing about nest boxes for barn owls is that they are often placed in the attics of farms and in church towers. Because these boxes are not hung up in trees, they are often made of material other than wood, such as pvc and cement. There are some other size models available as well: 19¾ by 19¾ by 27½ inches (50 × 50 × 70

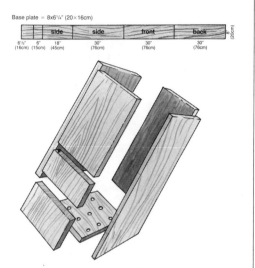

Base plate = 8x6¼" (20×16cm)

| side | side | front | back |

6½" (16cm) · 6" (15cm) · 18" (45cm) · 30" (76cm) · 30" (76cm) · 30" (76cm) · (20cm)

A chimney nest box is excellent for screech owls. Attach it with heavy gauge wire to the underside of a thick tree branch. A layer of peat on the bottom helps keep the box moderately clean. Note the little door in the lefthand side panel.

cm), and 19¾ by 15¾ by 17¾ inches (50×40×45 cm).

Barn Swallows

A simple 6 by 6 inch nest plank (15×15 cm), which has a lip of 3½ inches (8 cm) is all that is required. These swallows do not breed on the outside of houses, but always choose an inside location, in a barn, shed, or underneath a bridge, etc., so that mounting a simple nesting plank will be helpful to them. Affix a piece of fine aviary mesh to the upstanding edge to provide support when the birds build the nest. There are artificial nests available on the market that are a good imitation of the genuine article. These come already attached to a plank and can be placed in barns, sheds, chicken coops, etc.

Artificial Nests for Owls and Falcons

This type of nest is built up starting with a circular ring attached to a plank. Wire spokes are af-

fixed to allow the braiding of a basket. The larger openings between these spokes are filled in with aviary mesh. The basket is then finished by weaving thin twigs (preferably from the willow tree) between the spokes, after which the basket can be filled with grass, hay, leaves, moss, and similar materials.

Builder's Yard

In addition to specific nest boxes, consider providing a *builder's yard*. This is a supply cabinet with building materials for bird nests. It is built much like a shadow box, with some coarse wire or a few bars attached along the front. It is divided into four or more pigeon holes filled with hay, pieces of yarn (not too long, because the birds can become entangled in them), chicken feathers, dog hair, sheep's wool, horsehair, tiny scraps of material, shredded paper, bark fuzz, moss, dry leaves, hennep, string, etc. Hang up this builder's yard in a

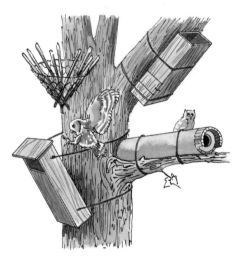

Various owl nests. Top left: a platform to assist the great horned owl. Top right and bottom: three safe ways of attaching nest boxes for screech owls and other small owl species.

Two barn-owl nesting trays; the top one has a lid to prevent adult owls from entering the hatchling's side of the tray. The ideal size: 37 inches long, 16 inches wide, and 12 inches high.

Top: sparrows will always try to take over the nests of cliff swallows. To prevent this in your artificial nests, attach 1-foot (30 cm) strings, weighted with a nut or bolt, to the eaves. The swallows fly up to their nests from below, but the sparrows, which fly vertically, will be put off. Middle and bottom: three artificial nests for barn swallows.

place where the contents will remain dry, and refill when necessary.

Sites for Nest Boxes

In general, the best locations for nest boxes are against walls and in trees. You can create some natural nesting locations by some artful pruning (see page 23), or you can place some artificial nests in those locations.

When choosing a place to hang your nest boxes, try to remember that they should not be accessible to cats and other predators. I like to stay within a range of 7 to 12 feet. The 7-foot low makes it a little more difficult for vandals with an interest in birds that lies on another plane than ours. The nest opening should face away from prevailing winds, directed toward the east or southeast, and in a way so that it will not be either too dark or too sunny inside the box. You might consider hanging the box

Open-fronted nest boxes for a kestrel, fixed on a 20 to 35-foot pole. Size: 25 by 15 by 15 inches, with roof overhanging approximately 3 inches.

Help With Nesting

A variety of wren nest facilities: top, a coconut and a pipe; middle, a wooden commercial wren nest box, and bottom, a flower-pot and a ceramic wren house.

somewhat tilted downward to prevent the rain from beating in, since this could wash away the entire brood of eggs or young. A piece of wood about an inch thick between the top of the nest box and the tree (or whatever you are hanging the box on) will provide a good tilt. Use waterproof covering materials for the roof, and let it extend a little in the front to keep hard rain and hot sun out of the box. This is particularly important with the so-called open front nest box. In the bottom of each nest box we should drill five to seven drainage holes. Nest boxes on tree trunks should have a flight path unhampered by a lot of twigs and leaves. To prevent squirrels, cats, and other bird enemies from climbing up to the nest boxes or feeders, fasten an 8 inch (20 cm) wide metal or plastic strip around the trunk or pole. Thorned or sharp twigs skirted around the trunk or pole will work very well, too. Or cut 3 inch (7 cm) wide strips from tin cans with points along one edge. Affix three or four of these strips, points down, about 5 inches (12 cm) away from each other. Once they are properly attached, you can bend the points out a little, and no cat, weasel, or any other bird enemy in its right mind will dare attempt to reach the nest box!

You can attach the nesting boxes against walls as well as trees, particularly the open-fronted ones, but choose the side of the wall with the least exposure to winds and rain. The south side should be picked only if the location is not too sunny. Under the eaves is a good location.

Caring for Injured and Orphaned Wild Birds

When you are involved in birding and are regularly confronted with birds in your backyard, sooner or later you will discover an injured or orphaned bird. What should you do? First of all, make sure the bird you found is really injured, and not just taking a little rest. Initially, keep your distance

Construction plan for a bluebird nest box, and a bluebird trail. Bluebirds, the harbingers of spring, readily use nesting boxes. The entrance should be 1½ inches in diameter, the floor 5 inches square, and the sides 10 inches, sloping to 9 inches in front. The boxes should be put on posts 5 to 6 feet above the ground, and approximately 30 feet apart.

Help With Nesting

To prevent damage to trees, use a leather strap to attach the nest box or a strip of leather to hang a bird feeder.

Always situate nest boxes facing away from prevailing winds and rains, and somewhat tilted, for obvious reasons.

and observe the bird. If it remains sitting on the same spot, without displaying any kind of activity, such as preening, alertly looking around, or hopping around occasionally, then it is indeed likely that the bird is sick or injured. If there is still enough life in him, and if it is a young bird, place it on a branch (because of the danger of cats). If it is a healthy and adult bird, it will undoubtedly take off as you approach.

A young bird that has left the nest too early or has fallen out of it must be placed back into the nest as soon as possible, because every hour that the bird does not get food from its parents leaves it weaker and reduces its chances of survival. An orphaned bird is generally very anxious and will sit very quietly waiting for its parents to find it. But often this does not happen, and it weakens even as you watch. If you should find such a bird, put it into the nest and see if indeed the parents accept and feed it. An orphaned bird can also be placed in a nest with other young birds of the same age and species. Generally, the foster parents will take care of the new addition. However, you should

The entrance to this nest box is protected by a metal strip (to keep off woodpeckers) and a metal basket (to keep out predators).

52

keep a careful eye on the situation, because if the parents have not fed the young bird after two hours, you may assume that it has been abandoned.

How to Handle an Injured Bird

An injured bird is best approached from behind. We recommend you wear lightweight cloth gloves, because once a bird has been picked up, its fear may well prompt it not only to struggle wildly, but to bite rather hard as well. If you are dealing with a bird of prey, use a jacket, blanket, or heavy towel and cover the victim with this completely. Sturdy leather gloves are no luxury, because birds of prey defend themselves with their razor-sharp talons. Once the bird has calmed down, pick it up so that its wings lie smoothly against its body. If the bird needs to be transported, use the above mentioned articles to form a sack, tying it at the top with a shoelace—something that is usually available. Keep the danger of overheating in mind, because

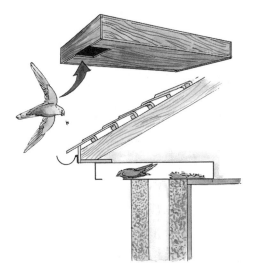

A swift nest box should be situated below the eaves in the loft. The box should measure 20 by 8 by 5 inches, with an entrance hole 5 by 3 inches, made in the *floor*.

this can happen very readily on warm summer days. Use a cardboard box or shoe box in which you have punched some air holes if circumstances permit. Put some pine shavings, cedar shavings, or shredded newspaper in the box if any of these are available. If you are dealing with a bird that has broken bones, such material can offer at least some exterior support. Take great care when carrying or moving the box.

How to Care for an Injured Bird

• Provide adequate warmth. Use a towel or blanket in cold weather.
• Take great care in handling an injured bird.
• An injured bird should be given species-appropriate food. The shape of its beak (see page 31) is a good indication of the type of food it normally eats.
• Take the bird immediately to an avian veterinarian, and if there is none present in your vicinity, take the bird to one of the following:

Zoo
Audubon Society
Department of fish and game
Humane organizations
Natural history museum
Wildlife rehabilitation groups

Keep in mind that many wild birds are protected under federal and state laws, and it is often illegal to be in possession of such a bird without the necessary license. So if you come across an injured wild bird, call one of the organizations listed and inquire what the best method of handling this matter might be.

How to Care for an Orphaned Bird

• First of all, determine whether the bird has been injured. If so, follow the steps listed above.
• Keep the bird calm and warm—a temperature of 85 to 90°F (29–32°C). For very young birds, the required temperature is 95 to 97°F (35–36°C).
• Keep the bird in a cardboard box using wire mesh

as a roof. As bedding it is best to use cedar or pine shavings or shredded newspaper.

• Provide appropriate food (see page 31). It would not hurt to weigh the bird at regular intervals, and obviously, its weight should increase. It is also helpful to feel carefully the flesh on both sides of the brestbone (keel) with thumb and forefinger. If the flesh feels sturdy, then the bird is probably in good health. If it feels thin and loose, you will need to improve the feedings, and/or increase them. If a bird produces an average of 22 droppings per day, it is probably in good health.

• Weak and cold young birds should initially be fed with a quart of water mixed with 3 teaspoons of honey to which one-half teaspoon of salt has been added. Administer about 20 drops every 15 minutes. The food should be about 100°F (38°C). The bird itself should also be kept warm. By using an infra-red lamp, you can maintain a temperature of about 92°F (33.3°C). You can feel with your hand if the glow is too warm. Place the lamp so the bird can move out of the rays if it wants to.

• When the orphaned bird is eating properly, we can start to add Avi-start or a similar special bird formula to this mixture. These foods, readily available in the better pet shops, are also used for rearing all kinds of pet birds. Detailed instructions are in-

cluded with the products. In the event that a special bird formula is not available, use canned dog food, baby food, etc.

Feeding Techniques:

• Add warm (100–110°F [38–43°C]) bottled (not distilled) water or apple juice to the formula.

• Mix formula well until it has the consistency of creamy milk. Never administer the formula too thick because it will congeal in the crop and will be unable to pass into the stomach. By giving the bird lukewarm water and some gentle crop massaging, this problem can easily be corrected. If, however, the crop remains full or is not emptying correctly, there could be a digestive problem. Consult an avian veterinarian or an experienced bird breeder immediately.

• Draw formula into a plastic eye dropper or syringe or let it roll off a teaspoon, the sides of which have been bent inward—the feeding tool we like best. The feeding utensil should be as close to the temperature of the formula as possible: 100–110°F (38–43°C).

• Use one feeding instrument and one feeding dish per bird. Never dip a feeding instrument into the food dish of another bird after it has touched the first bird's mouth. Sterilize your feeding instrument after every feeding.

• Maintain the right temperature for the formula during the whole feeding process by placing the dish with bird formula in a pan of warm (100–110°F [38–43°C]) water.

• Place the bird on a flat surface on a bath towel that feels warm to the touch.

• When a baby bird doesn't want to open its beak (gape), tap it gently on the beak with the feeding utensil. This will encourage the baby bird to gape.

• Examine the bird's crop before each feeding to determine the frequency and volume of the feeding. Remember, a crop should never become completely empty. Usually the crop will empty itself in 3½ to 4 hours.

• Don't overfill the crop. Overfilling can lead to backflow up the gullet (esophagus), into the throat, and down the windpipe, and so kill the bird.

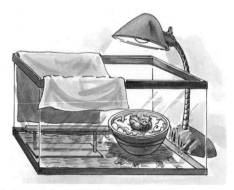

Orphan baby birds should be kept warm at 95 to 97° F (35–36° C), and fledglings that have some feathers should be kept at 85° to 90° F (29–32° C).

Help With Nesting

By far the best feeder is a thin, round-tipped spatula cut from a wooden match stick. This makes it possible to push the food to the back of the youngster's tongue and near the entrance of the gullet.

• Always determine the fullness of the bird's crop. Stop feeding immediately when the food is flowing back into the mouth. Don't resume feeding until the mouth is completely empty again.

• Feeding has to be synchronized with swallowing. As soon as the baby bird swallows—which goes with a rhythmic bobbing of the head—deliver the formula quickly. Place the feeding device into the mouth over the tongue.

• Support the bird, while feeding, with a cupped (and warm) hand.

• After each feeding, rinse the bird's mouth with a few drops of warm (100–110°F [38–43°C]) water.

• After each feeding, clean the bird's beak, head and other body parts, including the anus (vent), with lukewarm water and return the bird to its warm (90–95°F [32–35°C]) quarters.

Hatching to one week: A baby bird, depending on the species, can be removed from its parents after 10 to 21 days, or when the chick is just starting to feather. The later the safer. However, when you must hand-feed a hatchling, note the following: Don't feed a hatchling for the first 10 to 15 hours. Then start with one drop of lukewarm water. After one hour, another drop. Thereafter, a few drops of very thin formula every hour around the clock.

One to two weeks: Feed every 2 to 3 hours around the clock. If the birds are properly housed (warm and comfortable, at a temperature of 90–95°F [32–35°C]), feeding after midnight can be eliminated until 5 AM. The formula must now have the consistency of light cream.

Two to three weeks: Feed every 3 to 4 hours from 5 AM to midnight. Continue a formula consistency of light cream.

Three to four weeks: Feed every four hours with a slightly thicker formula with a consistency of heavy cream. Birds must be housed in a cage with low perches and a shallow bowl of water.

Five to six weeks: Feed a formula with the consistency of light cream. Introduce free choice of sprouted seeds and millet spray, or whatever is required to encourage the baby bird to forage on its own. Mix some formula with the food.

Seven to eight weeks: Feed the formula once a day. House the baby bird in a large cage with proper food cups and water bowl.

Common Visiting Birds

Wood Duck (*Aix sponsa*)
Family: Ducks (*Anatinae*)

Identification: 18½ inches (46.5 cm). Male: striped face with green, purple, and white. Brown throat and upper breast. White underparts. Gray-green flanks. Beak red with black tip. Female: dark brown with grayish underparts. White area around the eye.

Habitat: woodland streams, ponds, swamps, marsh, and other waters.

Nest: in a cavity in a tree trunk or limb (from woodpecker, for example), or nest boxes. Lined with down.

Breeding season: from April in the southern region to May in north of range.

Eggs: white or creamy; glossy.

Incubation: 28 to 37 days. Only the female incubates.

Nestlings: precocial. The young are cared for by the mother for up to 70 days. Nestlings leave the cavity or nest box in 24 hours. They have sharp claws and are able to climb up to 8 feet.

Food: seeds, grains, berries, aquatic inverts and terrestrial insects.

Range: southern Canada and eastern United States; also along the west coast, Texas, and Gulf coast.

American Kestrel (*Falco sparverius*)
Family: Falcons (*Falconidae*)

Identification: 10½ inches (25 cm). Male: upperparts reddish-brown; gray-blue wings. Gray forehead and reddish-brown crown. White face with two vertical black stripes before and behind the eye. Underparts whitish. Wings, flanks and back rufous-red with black spots or bars. Black subterminal tail band. Female: darker, with duller-colored head.

Habitat: open country with trees, woodland edges, parks, and gardens.

Nest: cavities or crevices, woodpecker's holes, or nest boxes. Sometimes in an old nest. No nesting material is used other than what is already in the nest.

Breeding season: from early March in the southern region to the end of May in north of range.

Eggs: 4 to 5, sometimes 3 to 7. White to pinkish. Tiny red-brownish specks and blotches.

Incubation: 29 to 30 days. The female mostly incubates alone, while foraged for by the male.

Nestlings: The young are cared for by both parents. They leave the nest at 30 days.

Food: insects, small vertebrates, small mammals (mice), and sometimes birds.

Range: throughout Canada, Alaska, and continental United States.

Northern Bobwhite (*Colinus virginianus*)
Family: Gamebirds (*Phasianidae*)

Identification: 9¾ inches (24.5 cm). Male: upperparts, flanks and upperbreast reddish-brown. Lighter underparts, which have dark spotting and scaling. White throat and stripe above the eye. Female: duller. Throat and eye-stripe buff-colored.

Habitat: brushy fields, farmland, grassland, woodland edges, large parks, and gardens.

Nest: on the ground, a shallow hollow, lined with grass. One brood per season.

Breeding season: from March in the southern region to the end of May in north of range.

Eggs: 12 to 16, sometimes 6 to 28. Whitish and somewhat glossy.

Incubation: 18 to 20 days. Young are independent as soon as they are born (precocial).

Nestlings: the young are cared for by both parents. The family stays together until the spring of next year.

Food: buds, leaves, seeds, insects, spiders, and snails.

Range: eastern United States, from southwest Maine and southern Ontario to the Gulf. Also some small areas in southern Washington and Wyoming.

Ring-necked Pheasant (*Phasianus colchicus*)
Family: Gamebirds (*Phasianidae*)

Identification: 33 inches (83.5 cm). Male: red facial patches. White ring around the neck. Dark brown breast. Reddish-brown overall. Long, pointed and curved tail. Female: brownish, with black and brown markings.

Habitat: woodland, near hedgerows, waste land, marsh land, farmland, parks and gardens. Females nest alone. Male is polygamous. Nest on the ground. Only one brood per season.

Nest: shallow depression in the ground, without any lining, or occasionally some leaves, grass, and plant fibers.

Breeding season: from early April to mid-May.

Eggs: 10 to 12. Glossy, olive brown or blue-gray.

Incubation: 23 to 25 days. The female incubates alone.

Nestlings: the young are precocial, and are cared for by the female (led to forage, etc.). Nestlings are able to fly in approximately 12 to 14 days.

Food: seeds, grains, insects, berries, fruits, and aquatic inverts.

Range: introduced from Asia. Various parts of the United States and along the Canadian border.

Common Ground Dove (*Columbina passerina*)
Family: Pigeons (*Columbidae*)

Identification: 6½ inches (16.5 cm). Adults: dark gray-brown upperparts and scalloping on head and breast; the latter is pinkish gray. Black wing spots. Reddish-brown on primaries, flashing in flight. Blackish back and tail, the latter with white spots at corners.

Habitat: open country, open woodland, parks, and gardens.

Nest: very flimsy platform, made of twigs, grass, rootlets, and sometimes small feathers.

Breeding season: from February to November. Three to four broods per season.

Eggs: Two. White and glossy.

Incubation: Two weeks. Incubated by both sexes.

Nestlings: the young are cared for by both parents. They leave the nest at 11 days.

Food: seeds, berries, buds, and sometimes insects and spiders.

Range: from southern California to the southern parts of the Gulf states. Also along the east coast to North Carolina.

Mourning Dove (*Zenaida macroura*)
Family: Pigeons (*Columbidae*)

Identification: 12 inches (30 cm). Adults: yellowish-brown head. Black spot below and behind the eye. Breast and belly pink-gray. Pointed, long pink tail with large spots flashing in flight.

Habitat: open woodland, farmland, parks, and gardens, usually near water.

Nest: thin, flimsy platform, made of twigs and grass. Lined with little twigs. Two, sometimes three broods per season.

Breeding season: from December to February in the southern region to late April in north of range.

Eggs: Two. White and glossy.

Incubation: 14 days. Both sexes incubate.

Nestlings: the young are cared for by both parents; they leave the nest at 12 to 14 days.

Food: seeds and grains.

Range: throughout the continental United States, Alaska, and Canada.

Barn Owl (*Tyto alba*)
Family: Owls (*Tytonidae* and *Strigidae*)

Identification: 16 inches (40 cm). Adults: heart-shaped face. Upperparts yellowish-buff, underparts white to reddish-brown, with little black spots.

Habitat: near trees and buildings, grassland, cliffs, and quarries.

Nest: in shallow cavities, lined with owl pellets, little sticks, and wood chips. Accepts nest boxes.

Breeding season: from January in the southern region to March in north of range. Sometimes two broods per season.

Eggs: Five to seven, sometimes three to 11. White and somewhat glossy.

Incubation: 30 to 34 days. The female incubates alone.

Nestlings: The young are cared for by both parents. They leave the nest at approximately 60 days. The barn owl is one of the few owl species with

Common Visiting Birds

two down coats: the first is short and whitish (absent on the back of the tarsus and on both sides of the neck), the second one (replaced after approximately 12 days) long and creamish down.

Food: rodents (voles), birds, insects, sometimes small reptiles and amphibians.

Range: throughout the United States, except the northern areas of the midwest.

Great Horned Owl (*Bubo virginianus*)
Family: Owls (*Tytonidae* and *Strigidae*)
Identification: 22 inches (55.5 cm). Adults: upperparts mottled gray-brown. Whitish throat collar. Brownish yellow underparts with little dark brown stripes. Large ear tufts. Light brown face.
Habitat: woodlands, swamps, orchards, parks, and gardens. Mainly nocturnal.
Nest: old (raptor) nest or cavity in tree, cave, wood stump, among rocks, etc. Only one brood per season.
Breeding season: from late November in the southern region to early April in north of range.
Eggs: Two to three, sometimes one to six. White and somewhat glossy.
Incubation: 30 to 35 days. The female incubates alone.
Nestlings: the young are cared for by both parents. They leave the nest at approximately 35 days. They fly poorly (at 60 to 70 days), and are looked after by both parents for several months.
Food: rodents (rabbits), birds (quail, finches), insects, reptiles, amphibians and scorpions.
Range: throughout Canada and United States.

Eastern Screech Owl (*Otus asio*)
Family: Owls (*Tytonidae* and *Strigidae*)
Identification: 8½ inches (21.5 cm). Adults: upperparts grayish-brown to brownish-red. White wing spots. Striped back. Underparts reddish-brown to gray, with thin bars. Small ear tufts.
Habitat: areas with trees, in gardens, parks, orchards, and groves.
Nest: usually in a tree cavity, woodpecker's hole or nest box. Lined with fur and feather debris.

Breeding season: from early March in the southern region to early May in north of range.
Eggs: Four to five, sometimes two to eight. White and somewhat glossy.
Incubation: approximately 26 days. The female incubates alone.
Nestlings: the young are cared for by both parents. They feed themselves at nine to 11 days and leave the nest after 20 days.
Food: small mammals, birds, insects, small vertebrates, fish, and arthropods.
Range: southern Canada to the Gulf and Florida.

Chimney Swift (*Chaetura pelagia*)
Family: Swifts (*Apodidae*)
Identification: 5¼ inches (13 cm). Adults: dark brown. Long wings, short tail.
Habitat: woodland, open farmland, and where human settlement occurs.
Nest: half-cup; made of dead twigs, which are glued together to a brick wall or chimney wall by a copious saliva secretion.
Breeding season: May.
Eggs: Four to five, sometimes three to six. White, unmarked and somewhat glossy.
Incubation: 19 days. Both sexes incubate.
Nestlings: the young are cared for by both parents. They leave the nest at 28 days.
Food: flying insects.
Range: southeastern Canada and eastern United States, from North Dakota to Newfoundland, south through Texas.

Ruby-throated Hummingbird (*Archilochus colubris*)
Family: Hummingbirds (*Trochilidae*)
Identification: 3¾ inches (19.5 cm). Male: upperparts green, underparts whitish. Tail black. Red throat. Female: white throat (gorget). Tail with white spots.
Habitat: near water, mixed woodland, parks and gardens.
Nest: cup-shaped; made from a variety of plant

Common Visiting Birds

materials, and lined with plant down. The whole structure is bound together with spider's webs, and "decorated" with lichens. Built by female.

Breeding season: from late March in the southern range to early June in north of range.

Eggs: Two. White, non-glossy; unmarked.

Incubation: 16 days. The female incubates alone.

Nestlings: the young are cared for by the female only. They leave the nest at approximately 19 days.

Food: nectar, insects, and spiders.

Range: Southern Canada and eastern United States, east of the Mississippi.

Black-chinned Hummingbird (*Archilochus alexandri*)
Family: Hummingbirds (*Trochilidae*)

Identification: 3¾ inches (19.5 cm). As the ruby-throated hummingbird, but with a black-violet throat.

Habitat: mountain areas, canyons, woodland edges, near water, in parks and gardens.

Nest: cup-shaped. Primarily made of plant down, and bound together with spider's silk. Built by female.

Breeding season: early April.

Eggs: Two, sometimes one or three. White, unmarked, and non-glossy.

Incubation: 13 to 16 days. The female incubates alone.

Nestlings: the young are cared for by only the female. They leave the nest at 21 days.

Food: nectar, insects, and spiders.

Range: western Great Plains.

Northern or Common Flicker (*Colaptes auratus*)
Family: Woodpeckers (*Picidae*)

Identification: 12½ inches (31 cm). There are three forms: male yellow-shafted flicker with yellow primary shafts, a black mustache, and a red patch on the back of the head; male red-shafted flicker, with reddish shafts to the primaries, a red mustache, and a red nape; and the third form, often called the gilded flicker, with yellow shafts to the primaries, and a red mustache. This last form is found in the southwestern portion of the United States. Further colors of the common flicker are: blue-gray crown, tan head with reddish eyebrow, gray wings with dark brown and black bars, a white rump and white flanks (with black spots), and a black breast spot (necklace). Underside light tan, also with black spots. Underside tail yellow, top black. Females don't have black or red mustache.

Habitat: wooded areas, parks, and gardens.

Nest: cavity in tree trunks, posts, telegraph poles, and nest boxes.

Breeding season: from early May in the southern region to June in north of range.

Eggs: Five to eight, sometimes three to 12. White, glossy and unmarked.

Incubation: 11 to 14 days; by both sexes. The female usually during the day.

Nestlings: The young are cared for by both parents. They leave the nest at 25 to 28 days.

Food: insects (ants) and spiders; sometimes seeds, nuts, and acorns.

Range: throughout the continental United States, Alaska, and Canada.

Hairy Woodpecker (*Picoides* or *Dendrocopos villosus*)
Family: Woodpeckers (*Picidae*)

Identification: 9¼ inches (23 cm). Adults: black upperparts, except for the back, which is white. White spots on wings. White underparts and outer tail feathers. White-and-black striped head. Black mustache. Males have a red patch on nape (young birds on crown).

Habitat: deciduous woodland, orchards, wooded swamps, parks, and gardens.

Nest: cavity in tree trunk or limb. Sometimes in nest boxes and poles. Excavated by both sexes in approximately 2½ to 3½ weeks. The nest cavity is often lined with wood chips.

Breeding season: from late March in the southern region to late May in north of range.

Eggs: Four, sometimes three to six. White and glossy.

Incubation: 11 to 12 days. Both sexes incubate.

Nestlings: the young are cared for by both parents; they leave the nest at 28 to 30 days.

Food: insects; during fall and winter acorns and other nuts.

Range: throughout Canada, Alaska and continental United States.

Red-headed Woodpecker (*Melanerpes erythrocephalus*)
Family: Woodpeckers (*Picidae*)

Identification: 9¼ inches (23 cm). Adults: red head, white underparts, black tail. Upperparts black. Large white wing patch.

Habitat: open country with trees (oak and beech), parks, and gardens.

Nest: cavity in barkless tree, large limb, fence, telegraph pole, or roof.

Breeding season: from late April in the southern region to mid-May in north of range. Often two broods.

Eggs: Four to five, sometimes three to eight. White and somewhat glossy.

Incubation: approximately two weeks. Both sexes incubate.

Nestlings: the young are cared for by both parents. They leave the nest at 27 to 30 days.

Food: omnivorous: insects, spiders, nuts, seeds, bird eggs, nestlings, mice, fruits, and berries.

Range: central and eastern United States. Not in southern Florida and Texas.

Downy Woodpecker (*Picoides pubescens*)
Family: Woodpeckers (*Picidae*)

Identification: 6¾ inches (17 cm). Adults: similar to hairy woodpecker; the smallest woodpecker in the United States.

Habitat: open woodland, riparian woodland, orchards, parks, and gardens.

Nest: cavity in dead wood. Excavated by both sexes in approximately two to three weeks. Lined with wood chips.

Breeding season: from April in the northern region to late May in north of range.

Eggs: Four to five, sometimes three to six. White and glossy.

Incubation: 12 days. Both sexes incubate.

Nestlings: the young are cared for by both parents; they leave the nest at 20 to 25 days.

Food: insects, spiders, fruits, and seeds.

Range: throughout Canada and the United States, except parts of Arizona, southern New Mexico and Texas.

Red-bellied Woodpecker (*Melanerpes carolinus*)
Family: Woodpeckers (*Picidae*)

Identification: 9¼ inches (23 cm). Male: black upperparts with white, small stripes. Grayish white rump and uppertail coverts. Red forehead, crown and nape. Cheeks grayish-white. Underparts whitish with a tinge of red on belly. Female similar to male, except for the head, which is gray except for crown and nape. Forehead sometimes with yellow or red.

Habitat: woodland, orchards, swamps, parks, and gardens.

Nest: cavity in dead trunk or large limb, nest boxes.

Breeding season: from March in the southern region to mid-May in north of range.

Eggs: Four to five, sometimes three to eight. White and glossy.

Incubation: 12 to 14 days. Both sexes incubate.

Nestlings: the young are cared for by both parents. They leave the nest at 24 to 27 days.

Food: insects, spiders, fruits (oranges), berries, nuts and seeds.

Range: from central Texas up to central South Dakota, eastward to Massachusetts, and down to Florida.

Least Flycatcher (*Empidonax minimus*)
Family: Tyrant Flycatchers (*Tyrannidae*)

Identification: 5¼ inches (13 cm). Adults: gray-brown upperparts. White-grayish underparts. Two white wing bars. Small eye ring.

Habitat: open deciduous and mixed woodland,

Common Visiting Birds

farmland, orchards, near lakes and rivers, gardens, and parks.

Nest: cup-shaped. Made of pieces of bark, weed stems, cotton, wool, grass, and compactly bound with cocoons and spider's webs. Lined with moss, plant down, grass, rootlets, and small feathers.

Breeding season: from late May to early June.

Eggs: Four, sometimes three to six. Creamy-white.

Incubation: 13 to 15 days. The female incubates alone, beginning with the third egg, occasionally fed by the male.

Nestlings: the young are cared for by both parents. They leave the nest at 12 to 16 days.

Food: insects, spiders and berries, sometimes some seeds.

Range: Canada and northeastern United States.

Eastern Kingbird (*Tyrannus tyrannus*)
Family: Tyrant Flycatchers (*Tyrannidae*)

Identification: 8½ inches (22 cm). Adults: black head, white underparts and throat. Black tail with white tip. Two white wing bars. The red crest is rarely displayed.

Habitat: farmland, woodland edges, gardens, and park.

Nest: deep cup-shaped. Large, loose of construction, and made of rootlets, grass, moss, twigs, straw and hair, sometimes small feathers and wool. Lined with fine grass, rootlets, and hair.

Breeding season: from May in the southern region to the end of May in north of range.

Eggs: Three to four, sometimes two to five. White to creamy-white; sometimes pinkish. Marked with red-brownish, purple-brown and blackish spots.

Incubation: 16 to 18 days. Both sexes incubate.

Nestlings: the young are cared for by both parents. They leave the nest at approximately two weeks, but both parents continue to forage the young for another month to six weeks.

Food: insects, and sometimes fruits.

Range: widespread throughout the United States and Canada; not in California and most western parts of Arizona.

Eastern Phoebe (*Sayornis phoebe*)
Family: Tyrant Flycatchers (*Tyrannidae*)

Identification: 7 inches (17½ cm). Adults: brown-grayish upperparts, lighter underparts. Dark wings and head.

Habitat: woodland edges, rocky areas, orchards, around farms, gardens, and parks. Breeds on a ledge of a building, under a bridge, in a bank, and other similar places.

Nest: cup-shaped; made of mud pellets, moss, rootlets, grass, and vines. Lined with grass, rootlets, and hair. Built in seven to 12 days.

Breeding season: from April in the southern region to mid-May in north of range.

Eggs: Four to five, sometimes three to eight. White, slightly glossy, usually unmarked, but sometimes with little brown spots.

Incubation: 14 to 16 days. The female incubates alone.

Nestlings: the young are cared for by both parents. They leave the nest at 15 to 17 days.

Food: insects, spiders, small fish and frogs, some seeds and berries.

Range: breed from central Canada east to New Brunswick, south to mid-Texas and Maryland. Winters from Delaware west to Oklahoma and south to Mexico, the Gulf states and Florida.

Purple Martin (*Progne subis*)
Family: Martins and Swallows (*Hirundinidae*)

Identification: 8 inches (20 cm). Male: black. Female: black-grayish upperparts and gray-white underparts, with red-brownish flanks.

Habitat: where human settlement occurs; open country, savanna, parks, and gardens, preferably near water.

Nest: in tree holes, nest boxes, etc. Made of plant fibers, grass, moss, leaves, feathers, bark pieces, mud pellets, etc. Built by both sexes.

Breeding season: from the end of March in the southern region to early June in north of range.

Common Visiting Birds

Eggs: Four to five, sometimes three to eight. White, without any markings.

Incubation: 15 to 18 days. The female incubates alone.

Nestlings: the young are cared for by both parents; they leave the nest at 24 to 31 days.

Food: insects.

Range: Central southern Canada and eastern United States, and parts of Washington and southern California; also in parts of Utah and Arizona.

Tree Swallow (*Tachycineta bicolor*)
Family: Swallows and Martins (*Hirundinidae*)

Identification: 5¾ inches (14.5 cm). Male: white underparts; metallic sheen on blue-green upperparts. Short, notched tail. Triangular black-brownish wings. Female: duller, and with darker upperparts.

Habitat: wood edges, preferably close to water, tundra edges, and open country.

Nest: cup-shaped; in tree holes (woodpecker's holes) and other cavities, nest boxes, and crevices in wooden buildings. Made of plant fibers and lined with small feathers.

Breeding season: from late April in the southern region to mid-May in north of range.

Eggs: Four to five, sometimes three to seven. White and glossy.

Incubation: 13 to 16 days, by both parents.

Nestlings: the young are cared for by both adults. They leave the nest at approximately 19 days.

Food: insects, spiders and sometimes berries (especially when insects are unavailable).

Range: breeds in Northern United States, Canada, and Alaska. Winters from Washington to New England and from the Carolinas to northern California.

Barn Swallow (*Hirundo rustica*)
Family: Swallows and Martins (*Hirundinidae*)

Identification: 6¾ inches (17 cm). Adults: metallic dark blue-green upperparts. Buff underparts.

Red-brownish throat and forehead. Females are generally duller. Deeply forked, long tail.

Habitat: near water and open country, parks and gardens.

Nest: cup-shaped, against a vertical surface, on ledges in barns, under bridges, and in similar places. Made of mud pellets and plant fibers.

Breeding season: from April in the southern region to early June in north of range.

Eggs: Four to five, sometimes three to eight. White and glossy, with some gray, brown or reddish markings.

Incubation: 14 to 16 days. The female incubates alone.

Nestlings: the young are cared for by both parents. They leave the nest at 17 to 24 days.

Food: insects, spiders, sometimes berries and seed.

Range: Canada, Alaska and continental United States, except Florida and Georgia.

Cliff Swallow (*Hirundo pyrrhonota*)
Family: Swallows and Martins (*Hirundinidae*)

Identification: 5½ inches (14 cm). Adults: underparts orange. Chestnut throat and forehead (the latter is often light buff). Square tail.

Habitat: cliff and rock-places, also near tall buildings, in parks and gardens.

Nest: round, and made of mud pellets, sometimes with hair and plant fibers. Nests in colonies.

Breeding season: from early April in the southern region to late May in north of range. Two broods per season.

Eggs: Four to five, sometimes three to six. Creamy-white with dark brown, reddish or purple markings.

Incubation: 16 days. The female incubates mainly alone.

Nestlings: the young are cared for by both par-

Above left: The orchard oriole.
Above right: The indigo bunting.
Below left: The evening grosbeak.
Below right: The American goldfinch.

ents. They leave the nest at 23 days, often returning to the nest for two to three days.

Food: insects, sometimes berries.

Range: Canada and United States.

Blue Jay (*Cyanocitta cristata*)
Family: Jays, Crows, and Magpies (*Corvidae*)
Identification: 11½ inches (26.5 cm). Adults: blue upperparts, light gray underparts. White and black bars on tail and wings. Black lore and necklace.

Habitat: woodland, orchards, gardens, and parks.

Nest: cup-shaped. Made of grass, rootlets, pieces of bark, paper, hair, wool, lined with rootlets, fine grass, and bark.

Breeding season: from mid-March in the southern region to early May in north of range.

Eggs: Four to five, sometimes two to six. Variable in color and very glossy. From pale green to blueish-green; marked with green, purple, brown and gray blotches.

Incubation: 16 to 18 days. The female incubates alone.

Nestlings: the young are cared for by both parents. They leave the nest at 17 to 21 days. They are independent in approximately 20 to 25 days.

Food: omnivorous: insects, inverts, carrion, bird eggs, nestlings, nuts, seeds, and fruits.

Range: Canada and eastern region of United States.

Black-billed Magpie (*Pica pica*)
Family: Jays, Crows, and Magpies (*Corvidae*)
Identification: 19 inches (48 cm). Adults: black

Above left: The white-throated sparrow (*Zonotrichia albicollis*). The male often sings his melancholy song at night.
Above right: The American tree sparrow (*Spizella arborea*) has a canary-like song with a somewhat metallic quality.
Center left: The fox sparrow.
Center right: The chipping sparrow.
Below left: The dark-eyed junco.
Below right: The rufous-sided towhee.

upperparts, head, breast and lower belly. White underparts and shoulders. Tapered, long tail.

Habitat: canyons, valleys near water, open spaces, large parks, and gardens.

Nest: usually in the top of a large tree, in a twig fork. Bulky, cup-shaped with a dome of large twigs. The nest is made from thorny twigs, and lined with cow dung and mud, grass, plant stems, and hair. Built in approximately 45 days, by both sexes.

Breeding season: from late March in the southern region to late May in north of range.

Eggs: Five to eight, sometimes up to ten or 12. Pale greenish-gray, with brown and gray markings.

Incubation: 16 to 18 days. The female incubates alone.

Nestlings: the young are cared for by both parents; they leave the nest at 22 to 28 days.

Food: omnivorous: insects, carrion, inverts, fruits, and seeds.

Range: Canada, Alaska, and western United States. Sometimes a yellow-billed magpie (*P. muttalli*) may be seen in the Sacramento Valley of California. Not along the coast.

Black-capped Chickadee (*Parus atricapillus*)
Family: Titmice and Chickadees (*Paridae*)
Identification: 5¼ inches (13 cm). Adults: black cap and throat (bib). White cheeks and breast. Grayish upperparts. Rusty flanks.

Habitat: forests, gardens, and parks.

Nest: a tree cavity; lined by both sexes with moss, feathers, hair, wool, spider's silk, cocoons, and plant down.

Breeding season: from April in the southern region to May in north of range.

Eggs: Six to eight, sometimes five to ten. White, with fine reddish-brown or purple spots.

Incubation: 12 to 14 days. The female incubates alone, while foraged for by the male. Incomplete clutches are usually covered with grass and other fine nesting material. When disturbed the brooding female hisses like a snake.

Nestlings: the young are cared for by both parents. They leave the nest at 14 to 18 days.

Common Visiting Birds

Food: insects, spiders, conifer seeds, and fruits.
Range: Canada, Alaska and northern region of United States.

Tufted Titmouse (*Parus bicolor*)
Family: Titmice and Chickadees (*Paridae*)
Identification: 6½ inches (16.5 cm). Adults: gray crest, gray underparts, and small black forehead. Underparts light gray. Rusty flanks. The birds from Texas have a darker crest and a grayish forehead.
Habitat: deciduous woodland, parks, and gardens.
Nest: in cavities (woodpecker's hole), lined with moss, grass, dead leaves, fur, wool and plant fibers. Twice I found pieces of snake skin.
Breeding season: from late March in the southern region to late April in north of range.
Eggs: Five to seven, sometimes four to eight. White to creamy, with reddish-brown, purplish-red and lilac spots.
Incubation: 13 to 14 days. The female incubates alone. Long-term pair bond.
Nestlings: The young are cared for by both parents, open their eyes at the age of six days, are fully feathered at 10 to 12 days, and leave the nest at 15 to 18 days.
Food: insects, spiders, seeds, and fruits.
Range: Eastern United States, from the east coast to southern Minnesota and western Texas. Not in southern Florida.

White-breasted Nuthatch (*Sitta carolinensis*)
Family: Nuthatches (*Sittidae*)
Identification: 5¾ inches (14.5 cm). Male: black crown and nape. Gray upperparts, white underparts, white face. Some brown on belly. Female is similar to male but with gray crown and nape.
Habitat: deciduous and conifer woodlands of mountain regions, also in parks, gardens, and orchards.
Nest: in cavities (woodpecker's hole), floored with dead leaves, strips of bark, hair, small feathers and lumps of earth, or a cup, made of bark, rootlets, fur, hair, feathers, leaves, and grass.
Breeding season: from mid-March in the southern region to late April in north of range.
Eggs: Five to nine, sometimes ten. White, glossy and with red, reddish-brown and purple markings.
Incubation: 12 days. The female incubates alone, while foraged for by the male.
Nestlings: the young are cared for by both parents. They leave the nest at 14 to 15 days.
Food: insects, spiders, and during the winter some nuts.
Range: from southern Canada to Florida and the Gulf states. Absent in central Wyoming to Texas and in some western mountain areas.

Red-breasted Nuthatch (*Sitta canadensis*)
Family: Nuthatches (*Sittidae*)
Identification: 4½ inches (11.5 cm). Male: black crown. Upperparts grayish blue, underparts reddish white. Black line through eyes, white eyebrow. Female: duller, with a grayish-blue crown.
Habitat: coniferous woodland, parks, and gardens.
Nest: in cavities, nestboxes, woodpecker's holes. Cup-shaped, made from rootlets, hair, grass, moss, and fur. Pine, fir, or balsam resin is smeared around the nest entrance by both sexes.
Breeding season: late April to early May.
Eggs: Five to six, sometimes four to seven. White, with reddish-brown or purple markings.
Incubation: 12 days. The female incubates alone.
Nestlings: the young are cared for by both parents. They leave the nest at 20 to 22 days.
Food: insects, spiders, and during the winter, conifer seeds.
Range: Canada, Alaska, and continental United States, except Florida and southern Texas.

Brown Creeper (*Certhia americana*)
Family: Creepers (*Certhiidae*)
Identification: 5½ inches (14 cm). Adults: dark

brown upperparts with brown-yellow streaks, whitish underparts. Thin white eyebrow. Thin curved beak.

Habitat: coniferous woodland, mountains, parks, and gardens.

Nest: between loose bark or, sometimes, in crevices in trees. Cup-shaped (like a hammock). Made of moss, twigs, bark, grass, pine, and other needles, lined with small feathers and bark pieces. Built by both sexes.

Breeding season: from early April in the southern region to late May in north of range.

Eggs: Five to six, sometimes three to nine. White and glossy. Marked with reddish-brown and pink spots.

Incubation: 14 to 15 days. The female incubates alone.

Nestlings: the young are cared for by both parents. They leave the nest at 14 to 16 days.

Food: insects, spiders, and during the winter some nuts and acorns.

Range: Canada, Alaska, and continental United States.

House Wren (*Troglodytes aedon*)
Family: Wrens (*Troglodytidae*)

Identification: 4¾ inches (12 cm). Adults: plain grayish-brown, with pale, white eyebrow. Fine black bars on lower belly. Thin beak, short tail.

Habitat: open woodland, parks, and gardens.

Nest: in cavities. The male often constructs various rough nests. It is possible that this species is usually polygamous, as many of these nests are finished and lined by various females. Nests are made of grass, leaves, stems, and fibers, lined with grass, hair, wool, small feathers.

Breeding season: from April in the southern region to late May in north of range.

Eggs: Six to eight, sometimes five to 12. White, glossy and marked with fine purple-reddish and brown spots.

Incubation: the female incubates alone.

Nestlings: the young are cared for by both parents. They leave the nest at 12 to 18 days.

Food: insects, spiders and inverts.

Range: Canada, Alaska, and continental United States. Winters in Florida, southern Georgia, the Gulf states and Texas panhandle to the southern coast of California.

Northern Mockingbird (*Mimus polyglottos*)
Family: Mockingbirds and Thrashers (*Mimidae*)

Identification: 10 inches (25.5 cm). Adults: grayish upperparts, lighter underparts. Tail and wings black; two white bars.

Habitat: open woodland, gardens and parks.

Nest: cup-shaped, bulky. Made of twigs, grass, string, wool, leaves, and weed stems, lined with grass, hair, plant down and rootlets.

Breeding season: from February in the southwestern region to late April in north of range.

Eggs: Three to five, sometimes six. Pale blue or greenish blue, with reddish or reddish-brown markings.

Incubation: Two weeks by the female only.

Nestlings: the young are cared for by both parents. They leave the nest at 12 to 14 days.

Food: insects (sowbugs), snails, berries, and other fruits.

Range: from southern Maine in an almost straight line to northern California, and south throughout the United States. Scattered populations in southern Canada.

Gray Catbird (*Dumetella carolinensis*)
Family: Mockingbirds and Thrashers (*Mimidae*)

Identification: 8½ inches (21 cm). Adults: dark gray. Crown and tail black. Red-brownish undertail coverts.

Habitat: near water, woodland borders, marshes, orchards, parks, and gardens.

Nest: cup-shaped, bulky. Made of grass, weed stems, and dry leaves, lined with pine needles, pieces of bark, rootlets, and hair.

Breeding season: early May.

Eggs: Four, sometimes two to six. Blue or green-blue.

Incubation: 12 to 13 days, by the female only.

Common Visiting Birds

Nestlings: the young are cared for by both parents. They leave the nest at nine to ten days.

Food: insects, spiders, and berries, sometimes fruits.

Range: southern Canada and United States, from western Washington in a straight line down to eastern Texas. Winters from southeastern Texas, Gulf States, Florida, and the Carolinas to southeast Virginia.

Robin (*Turdus migratorius*)
Family: Thrushes (*Muscicapidae*)

Identification: 10 inches (25.5 cm). Male: gray-brown above, with bright red underparts and white belly. Black head, with white spots around the eyes. White throat with black streaks. Yellow beak. Female: duller.

Habitat: thick undergrowth, open country, woodlands, parks, and gardens.

Nest: cup-shaped, untidy foundation of grass, twigs, weed stems, and strings, lined with mud and grass.

Breeding season: from April in the northern region to mid-May in north of range.

Eggs: Four, sometimes three to seven. Light blue, sometimes white.

Incubation: 11 to 14 days by the female only.

Nestlings: the young are cared for by both parents. They leave the nest at 14 to 16 days.

Food: insects, snails, earthworms, and fruits.

Range: Canada and United States.

Eastern Bluebird (*Sialia sialis*)
Family: Thrushes (*Muscicapidae*)

Identification: 7 inches (18 cm). Adults: blue. Breast and throat reddish brown, belly white. Females are duller, the back more brownish.

Habitat: open woodland, parks, gardens, and orchards.

Nest: cup-shaped. Made of twigs, grass, and weed stems, lined with grass and hair, sometimes feathers.

Breeding season: March to April.

Eggs: Four to five, sometimes two to seven. Pale blue, sometimes white.

Incubation: 12 days. Both sexes incubate, but the female more than the male.

Nestlings: the young are cared for by both parents. They leave the nest at 16 to 20 days.

Food: insects, earthworms, snails, and berries.

Range: from southeastern Canada and eastern United States from North Dakota south through mid-Texas.

Hermit Thrush (*Catharus guttatus*)
Family: Thrushes (*Muscicapidae*)

Identification: 6¾ inches (17 cm). Adults: upperparts brownish-olive. Reddish tail. Small white eye ring. Underparts light gray with dark spotted breast.

Habitat: coniferous woodlands, parks, and gardens.

Nest: cup-shaped, bulky. Made of weed stems, leaves, twigs, moss, grass, pieces of bark and mud, lined with grass, rootlets and leaves.

Breeding season: from mid-February to mid-May.

Eggs: Three to four, sometimes five to six. Light blue.

Incubation: 12 to 13 days, by the female only.

Nestlings: the young are cared for by both parents. They leave the nest at ten days.

Food: insects, spiders, earthworms, and fruits, especially in the winter.

Range: breeds from southern Canada to Virginia. Winters from Connecticut and the Ohio Valley to Florida and Gulf States through southern Texas and up along the California coast.

Ruby-crowned Kinglet (*Regulus calendula*)
Family: Old Warblers (*Sylviidae*)

Identification: 4¼ inches (11 cm). Adults: olive-gray upperparts. Two white bars on darker wings. Short dark tail. White eye ring. The male has a red crown patch, which is often concealed.

Habitat: coniferous woodland, gardens, and parks.

Common Visiting Birds

Nest: deep, cup-shaped. Made from moss, plant fibers, grass, pieces of bark, and *Usner* lichen, bound together with spider's webs, fur, and hair. Lined with feathers.

Breeding season: May to July.

Eggs: Seven to eight, sometimes five to 11. Creamy white to buffish-white, with brownish or red-brownish markings.

Incubation: approximately 15 days. The female incubates alone, while foraged for by the male.

Nestlings: the young are cared for by both parents. They leave the nest at 12 to 13 days.

Food: insects, spiders, berries, and sometimes seeds.

Range: breeds in Canada and Alaska, and migrates through northern states. Winters in Iowa and from Virginia southward.

Golden-crowned Kinglet (*Regulus satrapa*)
Family: Old Warblers (*Sylviidae*)

Identification: 4 inches (10 cm). Adults: olive gray above, paler underparts. Bright yellow crown patch (paler in female), bordered with black stripes. White eyebrow. Short dark tail. The dark wings have a white bar.

Habitat: coniferous woodland, parks, and gardens.

Nest: deep, cup-shaped, like previous species.

Breeding season: from April in the southern region to early June in the northern parts.

Eggs: Eight to nine, sometimes five to ten. Creamy white to muddy cream, with brown and pale markings.

Incubation: approximately 15 days. The female incubates alone, while foraged for by the male.

Nestlings: the young are cared for by both parents. They leave the nest at 14 to 19 days.

Food: insects, spiders, fruits and seeds.

Range: Canada and United States, except Florida and southern parts of Gulf states.

Cedar Waxwing (*Bombycilla cedrorum*)
Family: Waxwings (*Bombycillidae*)

Identification: 7¼ inches (18.5 cm). Adults:

brownish; yellowish on belly, and whitish on undertail coverts. Rump, tail, and wings are grayish. Red tips on secondary wing coverts. Tail tip has a bright yellow band. Black mask, touched with white.

Habitat: coniferous and birch forests, scrublands, parks, and gardens.

Nest: cup-shaped, bulky. Made of weed stems and grass, lined with pine-needles, wool, plant down, or grass.

Breeding season: from early June, depending on available food.

Eggs: Three to five, sometimes six. Pale blue with black and grayish markings.

Incubation: Two weeks by the female only.

Nestlings: the young are cared for by both parents. They leave the nest at 16 to 18 days.

Food: berries, flowers, insects, and fruits.

Range: Canada and United States, except the Sierra Nevada.

Red-eyed Vireo (*Vireo olivaceus*)
Family: Vireos (*Vireonidae*)

Identification: 6 inches (15.5 cm). Adults: olive-green above, lighter underparts. Gray crown, whitish eyebrow. A dark stripe goes straight through the eyes.

Habitat: deciduous woodlands, groves, gardens, and parks.

Nest: cup-shaped, attached to twigs at its rim. Made of bark strips, rootlets, and grass, bound together with caterpillars' and/or spiders' webs.

Breeding season: from May in the southern region to June in the northern parts.

Eggs: Four, sometimes three to five. White, with reddish-brown or black markings.

Incubation: Two weeks. Both parents incubate.

Nestlings: the young are cared for by both parents; they leave the nest at ten to 12 days.

Food: insects, spiders, snails, and fruits.

Range: breeds from southern Canada to Gulf states and Florida.

Yellow-rumped Warbler (*Dendroica coronata*)

Common Visiting Birds

Family: Warblers (*Parulidae*)

Identification: 5½ inches (14 cm). Male: gray, white, and black, with yellow rump patch. In spring and summer males have some yellow on crown and flanks. Females are duller and more brownish. In winter males too are dull and brownish, with less yellow. Cheeks brown. Black eye patch. No yellow in crown. There are two forms: the common eastern form "Myrtle," and the "Audubon" form in the west, with a yellow throat. This sub-species lacks the black patch behind the eyes.

Habitat: coniferous and deciduous woodland, open country, gardens, and parks.

Nest: cup-shaped. Made of moss, plant wool, grass, lichen, rootlets, and hair, lined with small feathers and hair.

Breeding season: from April to June.

Eggs: Four to five, sometimes three to five. White and glossy, with brown, gray, reddish-brown and purple markings.

Incubation: 12 to 13 days. The female incubates alone.

Nestlings: the young are cared for by both parents. They leave the nest at 12 to 14 days.

Food: insects, spiders, and sometimes berries, especially in fall and winter.

Range: breeds in Canada, Alaska, and continental United States from northern Minnesota south to northern Connecticut, northern Georgia, northern Michigan and central Minnesota. Winters from southern New England south through Florida, the Gulf states, and western Texas.

Yellow Warbler (*Dendroica petechia*)
Family: Warblers (*Parulidae*)

Identification: 5 inches (12.5 cm). Male: yellow, with olive tinge on wings and tail. Rusty stripes on underparts, especially the breast. Female: duller, but with yellow tail spots.

Habitat: swamps, near water, gardens, and parks (near berry patches).

Nest: cup-shaped. Made of plant fibers, plant down, grass, and wool, lined with plant wool and fibers, and sometimes even small feathers.

Breeding season: from April in the southern region to late May in north of range.

Eggs: Four to five, sometimes three to six. White, glossy and with brown, reddish brown or purple markings.

Incubation: 11 days. The female incubates alone.

Nestlings: The young are cared for by both parents. They leave the nest at nine to 12 days.

Food: insects, spiders; sometimes berries.

Range: Canada, Alaska, and continental United States, except Texas, the Gulf states, and Florida. Winters in Mexico, southern California, and Arizona.

American Redstart (*Setophaga ruticilla*)
Family: Warblers (*Parulidae*)

Identification: 5¼ inches (13.5 cm). Male: metallic black with orange wing, tail, and flank patches. Female: duller with gray and yellow patches.

Habitat: open or mixed woodland, gardens, orchards, parks, often near water.

Nest: cup-shaped. Made of plant and bark fibers, grass, rootlets, and spiders' webs, lined with grass, plant and bark fibers, birch bark, and hair.

Breeding season: from late May to early June.

Eggs: Four, sometimes three to five. White with a grayish or greenish tint, with brown, gray, and purple markings.

Incubation: approximately 12 days. The female incubates alone.

Nestlings: the young are cared for by both parents. They leave the nest at nine days.

Food: insects and spiders, sometimes seeds and berries.

Range: breeds from Alaska and southern Canada to northern Georgia and northern Gulf states, winters in southern Florida and south Texas.

Orchard Oriole (*Icterus spurius*)
Family: Blackbirds and Orioles (*Icteridae*)

Identification: 7¼ inches (18.5 cm). Male: dark rusty red with a black head, throat, back, tail and wings. Female: yellowish with greenish back and tail.

Habitat: gardens, parks, orchards, along watercourses, and in woodland.

Nest: cup-shaped. Made of grass, long stems, and fibers, lined with plant down.

Breeding season: from late April in the southern region to early June in north of range.

Eggs: Three to five. Pale blue, with blackish, brown-gray, and purple markings.

Incubation: 12 to 15 days. The female incubates alone, while foraged for by the male.

Nestlings: the young are cared for by both parents. They leave the nest when approximately 14 days old.

Food: insects, spiders, fruit, and sometimes tree blossoms.

Range: breeds from Minnesota, southeast Ontario, and southern New England to the Gulf states and Florida.

Northern Oriole (*Icterus galbula*)
Family: Blackbirds and Orioles (*Icteridae*)

Identification: 8¾ inches (22.5 cm). Male: yellow, with black head, throat, and back. White wing bar. Tail black with yellow outer feathers. Female: olive-gray, with yellow-orange underparts and two small white wing bars.

Habitat: orchards, deciduous forests, parks, and gardens.

Nest: a deep pouch, approximately 4 inches across. Made of long twigs, hair, vine, bark, and long fibers.

Breeding season: from April in the southern region to late May in north of range.

Eggs: Four to five. Pale blue, with blackish, purple, and gray markings.

Incubation: approximately two weeks. The female incubates alone, while foraged for by the male.

Nestlings: the young are cared for by both parents. They leave the nest at 12 to 14 days.

Food: insects, spiders, fruits, and buds.

Range: Canada and United States, except Florida.

Common Grackle (*Quiscalus quiscula*)
Family: Blackbirds and Orioles (*Icteridae*)

Identification: 12½ inches (32.5 cm). Adults: black with metallic sheen. Yellow eyes.

Habitat: open country, forests, groves, cultivated areas near water, parks, and gardens.

Nest: cup-shaped, loose, and bulky. Made of grass, stems, Spanish moss, pine needles and, in places close to the beach, seaweed. Lined with grass, rootlets, hair, sometimes small feathers and mud.

Breeding season: from late March in the southern region to mid-May in north of range.

Eggs: Four to five, sometimes six to seven. Pale blue with black and brown-purple bold markings.

Incubation: 12 to 14 days. The female incubates alone.

Nestlings: the young are cared for by both parents. They leave the nest at 16 to 20 days.

Food: insects, small fish and aquatic inverts, bird eggs and nestlings, seeds, fruits, acorns and nuts.

Range: breeds from British Columbia, Newfoundland south to central Colorado and southern Texas, Gulf states and Florida. Winters east from southern Minnesota down to eastern Texas, Gulf states and Florida, and up to southern New England.

Brown-headed Cowbird (*Molothrus ater*)
Family: Blackbirds and Orioles (*Icteridae*)

Identification: 7½ inches (19 cm). Male: black with metallic sheen. Dark red-brown head. Female: brownish gray.

Habitat: farmland, groves, parks, and gardens.

Nest: brood parasite. Principal hosts are various warbler species, finches, vireos, and flycatchers. Usually one egg per nest.

Breeding season: from early April in the southern region to mid-May in north of range.

Eggs: approximately 30 by one female in one season.

Incubation: 11 to 12 days.

Nestlings: the young leave the nest at ten days

but the host will continue to feed the youngsters for another fortnight.

Food: insects, spiders, snails, and seeds.

Range: Canada and United States.

Red-winged Blackbird (*Agelaius phoeniceus*)
Family: Blackbirds and Orioles (*Icteridae*)

Identification: 8¾ inches (22.5 cm). Male: black; brilliant red shoulder patch, edged below with yellow. Female: dark brown, with buff underparts, heavily streaked. Some have a red tinge to the shoulder and an orange throat.

Habitat: salt and freshwater marshes, swamps, wet meadows, some parks and gardens.

Nest: cup-shaped. Made of plant fibers, roots, grasses, and mud, lined with grass and thin rushes.

Breeding season: from late March in the southern region to late May in north of range.

Eggs: Four, sometimes two to six. Pale blue with black, brownish, purple and grayish markings.

Incubation: Ten to 12 days. Only the female incubates.

Nestlings: the young are cared for by both parents; they leave the nest at ten to 14 days.

Food: insects, spiders, and seeds.

Range: Canada and United States.

Purple Finch (*Carpodacus purpureus*)
Family: Finches (*Fringillidae*)

Identification: 6 inches (15 cm). Male: raspberry red on rump and head, lighter on back and breast. White belly. Both sexes are heavily brown-streaked. Female: whitish eyebrow; dark ear patch. White undertail coverts.

Habitat: gardens, parks, and open woodland.

Nest: cup-shaped. Made of grass, twigs, and rootlets, lined with wool, hair, and moss.

Breeding season: February to May.

Eggs: Four to five, sometimes three to six. Light blue, with black and purple markings.

Incubation: 13 days. The female incubates alone, while foraged for by the male.

Nestlings: the young are cared for by both parents. They leave the nest at 13 to 14 days.

Food: seeds, tree buds, insects, spiders, and fruits.

Range: Canada, eastern United States, Florida and central Texas.

House Finch (*Carpodacus mexicanus*)
Family: Finches (*Fringillidae*)

Identification: 6 inches (15 cm). Male: red with brown wings, and streaks on flanks and underside. Female: gray-brown, belly lighter with heavy streaks.

Habitat: gardens, parks, and open country.

Nest: cup-shaped. Made of and lined with little twigs, rootlets, grass, wool, and small feathers.

Breeding season: From late February in the southern region to mid-April in north of range.

Eggs: Four to five, sometimes two to six. Pale blue-white, with fine black and purple markings. Occasionally unmarked.

Incubation: approximately two weeks. The female incubates alone while foraged for by the male.

Nestlings: the young are cared for by both parents. They leave the nest at 11 to 19 days.

Food: seeds, buds, and occasionally insects and spiders.

Range: Southeast Canada and west coast of United States south to eastern and central Texas, and east to Nebraska. On the east coast around New York (where the species was introduced), in Michigan and Georgia.

Pine Siskin (*Carduelis pinus*)
Family: Finches (*Fringillidae*)

Identification: 5 inches (13 cm). Adults: dark streaked. Yellow band on wings, also some yellow on the tail base.

Habitat: coniferous or mixed forests, thickets, gardens, and parks.

Nest: cup-shaped. Made of twigs, grass, and rootlets, lined with fur, hair, small feathers, and rootlets.

Breeding season: May to June.

Eggs: Three to four, sometimes one to five. Light blue-green with black and lilac markings.

Incubation: 13 days. The female incubates alone, while foraged for by the male.

Nestlings: the young are cared for by both parents. They leave the nest at 14 to 15 days.

Food: seeds and some insects and spiders.

Range: Canada, Alaska, and the continental United States. Winters in Mexico.

Evening Grosbeak (*Coccothraustes vespertinus*)
Family: Finches (*Fringillidae*)

Identification: 8 inches (20.5 cm). Male: large yellow cone-shaped beak, yellow forehead, back, rump, and underside. Black wings with large white patches. Black tail. Female: yellowish brown. White markings in black tail and wings. Beak greenish yellow.

Habitat: spruce and coniferous forests, large gardens, parks, and residential areas.

Nest: cup-shaped, but loosely constructed. Made of and lined with moss, rootlets, lichen, hair, and fibers.

Breeding season: from mid-May in the southern region to early July in north of range.

Eggs: Three to four, sometimes two to five. Light blue or greenish-blue, with purple-brownish and green-brownish markings.

Incubation: 11 to 14 days. The female incubates alone, while foraged for by the male.

Nestlings: the young are cared for by both parents. They leave the nest at 13 to 14 days.

Food: seeds, insects (especially in the breeding season), berries (juniper), and nuts.

Range: Canada and United States. Not in Florida, along the Gulf or in southern California.

American Goldfinch (*Spinus* or *Carduelis tristis*)
Family: Finches (*Fringillidae*)

Identification: 5 inches (12.5 cm). Male: yellow, tail and wings black, forehead and crown also black. The wings have two narrow white bars. Female: brownish yellow. Clear yellow throat and breast. During the winter both sexes are light brownish with much white on the wings.

Habitat: gardens, parks, and groves, often near water or swamps.

Nest: cup-shaped. Made of plant fibers, roots, and strips of bark, lined with plant down.

Breeding season: from April/May in the southwestern region to mid-June in east of range.

Eggs: Four to six. Pale blue or green.

Incubation: 10 to 12 days. The female incubates alone, while foraged for by the male.

Nestlings: The young are cared for by both parents. They leave the nest at 11 to 17 days.

Food: seeds, berries, insects, and spiders.

Range: Canada and United States.

Northern Cardinal (*Cardinalis cardinalis*)
Family: Grosbeaks, buntings, and sparrows (*Emberizidae*)

Identification: 8¾ inches (22.5 cm). Male: red. Black face and throat. Red, pointed crest and beak. Female: gray-olive above, yellow-brown underparts. Some red in tail, wing and crest. Beak pink.

Habitat: woodland edges, open woodland, thickets, near streams, gardens, and parks.

Nest: cup-shaped. Made of grass, rootlets, dead leaves, pieces of paper, weed stems, lined with rootlets, hair, and grass.

Breeding season: from late March to April, three to four broods per season.

Eggs: Three to four, sometimes two to five. Whitish or greenish with dark brown, sometimes grayish, green, purple and reddish markings.

Incubation: 11 to 13 days. Usually by the female only.

Nestlings: the young are cared for by both parents. They leave the nest at nine to 11 days, and are independent at approximately 40 days.

Food: insects, spiders, seeds, and fruits.

Range: Throughout the United States, especially from New York to southern Minnesota, and down to Colorado and southwestern Texas.

Indigo Bunting (*Passerina cyanea*)
Family: Grosbeaks, buntings, and sparrows (*Emberizidae*)

Identification: 5½ inches (14 cm); smaller than the blue grosbeak. Male: blue; in autumn like the female, except for some blue in the wings and tail. Female: brown, with faint streaks on upper-breast, and some blue in the tail.

Habitat: Forest edges, scrub lands, fields, open woodland, hedgerows, parks, orchards, and gardens.

Nest: cup-shaped, in tree tangles or bush, about 3½ feet (1 meter) from the ground. Made of bark strips, cotton thread, wool, dried grass and weed stems, leaf veins, leaf fibers, Spanish moss, small feathers, spider webs, pieces of paper, and sometimes snakeskin; lined with rootlets, wool, grass, small feathers, (horse) hair, and cotton. The hen selects the site and builds the nest, although the male will bring her nesting material.

Breeding season: from mid-May to early June. Two broods.

Eggs: Three to four; sometimes two. Bluish or light green-white; unmarked.

Incubation: 12 to 13 days. Only the female incubates.

Nestlings: the young are cared for mainly by the female. Fledglings leave the nest at 9 to 13 days. The male sometimes feeds fledged young, when the hen starts a new nest and clutch.

Food: insects, seeds, and fruits.

Range: from Canada, eastern United States and Mexico, as well as Central America to Panama, Cuba, and the Bahamas. Indigo buntings breed only in northeastern United States and eastern Canada. At the end of September they migrate to the south, sometimes in very large flocks that stay together in their winter abodes. They are usually found only in pairs in their breeding locations, where they live a somewhat timid and withdrawn existence. The males sing often and long, though their song is comparatively simple and monotonous.

Song Sparrow (*Melospiza melodia*)
Family: Grosbeaks, buntings, and sparrows (*Emberizidae*:
Identification: 6¼ inches (16 cm). Adults: light brown with dark brown stripes on the back. Whitish eyebrow, dark mustache. Underside whitish-gray with dark breast stripes and often a central breast spot.

Habitat: swamps, thickets, brushy open country and farmland, gardens, and parks.

Nest: cup-shaped. Made of weed stems, leaves, and grass, sometimes rootlets and pieces of bark, lined with grass and hair.

Breeding season: early April.

Eggs: Three to five, sometimes two to six. Pale white-blue or greenish blue, with fine red-brownish, purplish or pale lilac markings.

· *Incubation*: Two weeks. The female incubates alone, while foraged for by the male.

Nestlings: the young are cared for by both parents. They leave the nest after ten days and are able to fly excellently when approximately 17 days old.

Food: seeds, insects, spiders, and sometimes berries.

Range: Canada, Alaska, and continental United States.

Fox Sparrow (*Passerella iliaca*)
Family: Grosbeaks, buntings, and sparrows (*Emberizidae*)
Identification: 7 inches (18 cm). Adults: reddish brown above with dark stripes. Underside whitish with red brown streaks and a central breast spot.

Habitat: cultivated and cleared areas, forest undergrowth, woodland thickets, and mountain brushland, some parks and gardens.

Nest: cup-shaped. Made of grasses, weed stems, pieces of bark, and sometimes rootlets, lined with fine grass and some hair and fur.

Breeding season: early April.

Eggs: Three to five, sometimes two to six. Pale blue-white or green-blue; marked with fine red-brownish, purplish, reddish or lilac markings.

Incubation: Two weeks, by mostly the female.

Nestlings: the young are cared for by both parents. They leave the nest when approximately 12 days old.

Food: seeds, berries, insects and spiders, buds, and sometimes berries.

Range: Canada and the western parts of United States. Winters in Ohio and Massachusetts to the Gulf states, through southern Texas and the California coast.

Chipping Sparrow (*Spizella passerina*)

Family: Grosbeaks, buntings, and sparrows (*Emberizidae*)

Identification: 5½ inches (14 cm). Adults: light red-brownish crown. Two dark forehead stripes, with white in the middle. Light brown above with dark stripes. Dark gray rump. Light gray undersides.

Habitat: open woodland, brushy open country, parks, and gardens.

Nest: cup-shaped, made of grass, little roots, and weed stems, lined with hair, fur and fine grass.

Breeding season: from mid-March in the southern region to early June in north of range.

Eggs: Four to five. Light blue, with blackish, brownish and pale blue markings.

Incubation: 11 to 12 days. The female incubates alone while foraged for by the male.

Nestlings: the young are cared for by both parents. They leave the nest at approximately nine to 12 days, and are able to fly after two weeks.

Food: insects, spiders, and seeds.

Range: Canada, Alaska, and continental United States. Winters in Florida and southern Texas.

Dark-eyed Junco (*Junco hyemalis*)

Family: Grosbeak, buntings, and sparrows (*Emberizidae*)

Identification: 6¼ inches (16 cm). Male: slate-colored, with white outer tail feathers and white belly. Female: duller, with brownish head, back, and tail.

Habitat: forest edges, open woodland, gardens, and parks.

Nest: cup-shaped. Made of grass, thin twigs, pieces of bark, moss, and rootlets, lined with hair, grass, and stems.

Breeding season: from mid-March in the southern regions to mid-May in north of range.

Eggs: Three to five, sometimes six. Greenish-white or grayish, with brownish-red and purple-brown markings.

Incubation: 11 to 12 days. The female incubates alone.

Nestlings: the young are cared for by both parents. They leave the nest at ten to 13 days.

Food: seeds, insects, and spiders.

Range: Canada, Alaska, and continental United States.

Rufous-sided Towhee (*Pipilo erythrophthalmus*)

Family: Grosbeaks, buntings, and sparrows (*Emberizidae*)

Identification: 8½ inches (21.5 cm). Male: black head, throat, and upperparts. Red-brownish flanks. White breast, belly, and tail edges. Female: duller, and brown instead of black.

Habitat: forest, low shrubby growth, parks, and gardens.

Nest: cup-shaped. Made of grass, pieces of bark, dead leaves and rootlets, lined with hair and grass.

Breeding season: late April to early May.

Eggs: Three to four, sometimes two to six. White or greenish. Reddish-brown, brown, or brown-grayish markings.

Incubation: 12 to 13 days. Only the female incubates.

Nestlings: the young are cared for by both parents. They leave the nest at ten to 12 days.

Food: insects, fruits (berries), and seeds.

Range: United States, except Texas and Oklahoma.

Index

Page numbers in *italics* indicate color photos, C2 indicates inside front cover; C3, inside back cover; C4, back cover.

Index

Index

Index

Useful Publications and Addresses

Books

American Favorite Backyard Birds by Kit and George Harrison (Simon & Schuster, New York)

An Audubon Handbook (2 volumes: *Eastern Birds, Western Birds*) by John Farrand, Jr. (McGraw-Hill Book Company, New York)

The Audubon Society Guide to Attracting Birds by Stephen W. Kress (Charles Scribner's Sons, New York)

The Backyard Bird Watcher by George H. Harrison (Simon & Schuster, New York)

The Birder's Handbook by Paul R. Ehrlich, David S. Dobkin, and Darryl Wheye (Simon & Schuster, New York)

The Birdhouse Book by Don McNeil (*Oregon Coast Magazine*, P.O. Box 18000, Florence, Oregon 97439)

Classic Architectural Birdhouses and Feeders by Malcolm Wells (Malcolm Wells, 673 Satucket Road, Brewster, Mass. 02631)

A Field Guide to the Birds (3 volumes: *Eastern Birds, Western Birds, Birds of Texas*) by Roger Tory Peterson (Houghton Mifflin Company, Boston)

A Field Guide to Birds' Nests by Hall H. Harrison (Houghton Mifflin Company, Boston)

Home for Birds Conservation Bulletin #14 of the U.S. Department of the Interior Fish and Wildlife Service (Superintendent of Documents, U.S. Government Printing Office, Washington, D.C. 20402; Stock Number 024-010-00524-4; price $2.50)

Stokes Nature Guides (3 volumes: *Bird Behavior*) by Donald and Lilian Stokes (Little, Brown and Company, Boston, MA)

Summer Bird Feeding by John V. Dennis (Audubon Workshop, 1501 Paddock Dr., Dept. 3113, Northbrook, IL 60062)

Magazines

Birding News Survey
Avian Publications, Inc.
P.O. Box 310
Elizabethtown, KY 42701

The Bird Watch
Bird Populations Institute
P.O. Box 637
Manhattan, KS 66502

Bird Watcher's Digest
P.O. Box 110
Marietta, OH 45750

WildBirds
P.O. Box 6050
Mission Viejo, CA 92690